DYNAMIC PORTFOLIO MANAGEMENT

The Bargery Fabrics Case

*Develop a dynamic portfolio of new products
that embraces evolving customer demands
and enhances company strategy*

Roger Warburton
Stephen Kay

RW PRESS

nw texnet
advanced flexible materials

Published in the United States of America by *RW-Press*, Newport, RI.

First Edition

> Version: 1.0c, May, 2018.

> Version: 1.0d, June, 2018.

ISBN: 978-0-9831788-9-7

Cover:

The cover's background image was supplied by Dr. Luis Felipe Padilla-Vaca, who is a Professor at the University of Guanajuato, Mexico. The image is from the Antimicrobial Coatings for the Textile Industry (ACTIN) project.

ACTIN is a collaborative effort between Mexican and UK companies and research institutes tasked with the development of durable anti-microbial textiles for the health care industry and is supported by Innovate UK's Newton Fund.

RW-Press
150 Eustis Avenue,
Newport, RI 02840. U.S.A.

www.RW-Press.com

To Eileen and Katharine

CONTENTS

8 Research   **83**

LIST OF FIGURES

LIST OF TABLES

PREFACE

Effective portfolio management is a competitive weapon.

And yet, a decade after we first developed the *Bargery Fabrics Case*, there is still a dearth of cases available for teaching this essential skill. This deficit appears in companies, where potential learners need practical guidance in the implementation and management of a portfolio, and in traditional academic courses, where faculty require cases that teach these valuable skills to students.

We attribute the lack of cases to the understandable reluctance of companies to discuss publicly their successes and, especially, their failures. While many books explain what makes a portfolio successful, there are few practical exercises for either company learners or students to develop their skills by working through a realistic scenario.

Historically, Product Portfolio Management (PPM) focused on selecting new products based on their projected financial rewards. The situation changed dramatically during the 1990s, when PPM research identified the factors critical to the success of new products.[1] The research, which was validated in companies in many business sectors and all over the world, laid the foundation for techniques that are both easy-to-understand and effective. [1]

More recently, there is a growing acceptance that portfolios are dynamic and that processes are required to adapt the portfolio continuously to product evolution and external business uncertainties. *Dynamic Portfolio Management* (DPM) enhances PPM by adding techniques that focus product selection towards achieving a company's *strategic* goals and objectives. [2]

In companies, the development of portfolio management processes requires a realistic assessment of the company's historical products, both successes and failures. However, employees are often reluctant to speak honestly about their company's previous failures, especially if they were involved in the product's development. Therefore, we have found that in order to teach portfolio management

[1] Interestingly, financial rewards turned out to be one of the poorest methods for selecting successful products.

effectively, one must first establish a safe environment for the discussion of a company's product history.

We provide that safe environment by having company learners first work through the *Bargery Fabrics Case*, which removes all personal aspects from the product evaluation discussion. Once the vocabulary and processes are understood, we have found that learners are then comfortable performing a realistic evaluation of their own company's previous successes and failures. Learners often realize, for example, that product failures were not due to their personal mistakes, but to a lack of appreciation of the importance of the critical success factors.[2] Therefore, first working through the *Bargery Fabrics Case* provides a safe, impartial environment for learning how to implement portfolio management.

Developing a portfolio management system using the company's own products proceeds more smoothly and much faster *after* running the *Bargery Fabrics Case* in a company training session. Therefore, while it may appear that running the *Bargery Fabrics Case* adds time to portfolio training, in fact, the time spent on the case results in improved understanding of the concepts and a more effective embedding of the processes in the company.

Dynamic Portfolio Management is soundly based on the latest research. The book teaches both learners in companies and students in the classroom how to evaluate and select potential new products, how to manage a dynamic portfolio, how to develop a roadmap for future product development, how to ensure that the selected new products accomplish the company's strategy, and how to embed new product development processes into the company's management structure.

Evolution of the *Bargery Fabrics Case*

In 2008 the authors developed a training course in New Product Development (NPD) that was delivered to companies throughout the North West of England, U.K. The course was part of the Advanced Skills for Advanced Materials (ASAM) Program, which was targeted to companies in the Advanced Flexible Materials (AFM) business sector.

ASAM was born out of an interesting and valuable piece of research conducted by the U.K. consultancy, David Rigby Associates, which found that many companies in the AFM sector could improve their performance by getting a better return on their investment in new products and developing a carefully considered outsourcing strategy, which we dubbed "balanced sourcing."

We viewed the integration of new product development and balanced sourcing

---

[2] Phew. It isn't about me.

as both innovative and critical. For companies to survive and prosper, they must innovate at the front end (new product development), while, at the same time, remain competitive at the back end (balanced sourcing). The ASAM program trained companies in all these processes.

The ASAM NPD training module was based on Robert Cooper's foundational research in Product Portfolio Management. [1] It was innovative in that it consisted of two days of in-company training by a team consisting of an experienced trainer and a subject matter expert.[3] The training was followed by several days of coaching by the subject matter experts and spreading the coaching over time enhanced the embedding of the newly learned techniques into the company's management processes.

The North West Development Agency (NWDA) set the goal that ASAM should improve the Gross Value Added (GVA) of our clients by £5 for every £1 spent on the program.[4] In fact, even after removing a couple of extraordinarily successful outliers, the average GVA of our clients improved by over £20 for every £1 spent.

As part of the NPD module, a teaching case in Product Portfolio Management (PPM) was developed that was targeted specifically towards companies in the AFM sector. During the very first running of the case in a commercial company, after the selection matrix was developed and displayed, there followed a minute of silence before the Marketing Director spoke up:

> "If we'd done this last year, we would not have lost our shirt on that dog at the bottom of the list."[5]

At that point, we knew that PPM worked. We also confirmed that what would become the *Bargery Fabrics Case* was a valuable and essential component of the training. Since then, we have taught portfolio management, based on the *Bargery Fabrics Case*, to more than 200 learners in 30 companies. Some comments from the learners were:

- "The number of products that exceed sales and profit targets has risen."

- "We have improved success rates and time to product launch is down."

- "We have better coordination between marketing and manufacturing."

- "Customer acceptance levels are higher at launch."

- "We have fewer design changes late in the product cycle."

[3]The team approach provided a balance between interesting presentations and the exacting technical demands of sophisticated AFM companies.

[4]GVA attempts to measure economic activity from the producer's side and is designed to help policymakers formulate sector-specific economic strategies.

[5]This was the origin of "kill the dogs."

- "Checkpoint gates are the key to spotting failures early."

While we always felt that that the *Bargery Fabrics Case* played an important role in a training course in portfolio management, it was only after several successful implementations that we began to realize just how important the case was in creating the safe, neutral environment essential to the assessment of a company's own products.[6]

The success of the *Bargery Fabrics Case* in commercial companies motivated us to explore the possibility of using it in the classroom in a project management curriculum where portfolio management is an important component. Adaptation to the classroom required the simplification of the portfolio's products so that no previous technical experience or knowledge was required by the students.

For the past seven years, the case has been taught several times each year during graduate courses in Project Management at Boston University's Metropolitan College (MET).[7] We include the *Bargery Fabrics Case* in graduate courses in Project Management (PM) and successfully present it in a single 3-hour class.[8]

The simplification of the portfolio had immediate benefits. The case is now completely general and, since the case no longer requires up-front knowledge about advanced materials, it can be run in any company in any business sector. As a result, we now use the identical *Bargery Fabrics Case* in companies and in the classroom.

While the case was successful, both in companies and in the classroom, we often felt that it seemed somewhat unfinished. This was particularly true about the final exercise—the strategic assessment of the portfolio. There was no formally validated method for determining if the selected products met the strategic goals of the company, which made the final assignment somewhat *ad hoc*.

The solution to this problem appeared in 2012 when Petit and Hobbs published their research monograph, *Project Portfolios in Dynamic Environments*. [2] This research formalized the idea that portfolios are dynamic and that they must adapt to changes and uncertainties. Petit and Hobbs defined a nomenclature that describes the evolution and transformation of a portfolio and proposed tools for evaluating its dynamic nature. They also defined the roadmap, which describes the evolution of the new products over time. From our perspective, Petit and Hobbs provided the critical missing piece for the *Bargery Fabrics Case*: a research-validated, formal method for the strategic assessment of a portfolio.

Therefore, we added the dynamic capabilities of Petit and Hobbs to the *Bargery Fabrics Case* and, as a result, it faithfully represents the characteristics of *Dynamic*

[6] We began referring to the case as portfolio management *detox*.

[7] BU's MET College prepares non-traditional students for the competitive and evolving needs of today's world.

[8] MET graduate students are non-traditional students—working professionals—who have a lot in common with learners in companies.

Portfolio Management (DPM) found in real companies. Once a company's staff has completed the *Bargery Fabrics Case*, they can move on to developing their own genuinely dynamic portfolio of new products.

Acknowledgments

Chris Byrne wrote an early version of this case that was targeted to companies in the AFM business sector. Chris deserves credit for developing the original product list, which was sophisticated enough to include most of the subtleties and complexities of real portfolios, while simple enough to be interesting and understandable.

The U.K.'s North West Development Agency provided the financial support for the development of the ASAM training program. The Manchester College financially supported the development of the DPM course upgrades.

Both authors are sincerely grateful to Mike Bentley for his friendship, his support, and his unfailing optimism. Mike provided invaluable help and support in recruiting the associates who delivered the ASAM training to companies, in marketing know-how to persuade companies to sign up for the program, and in hands-on project management. Mike has also contributed significantly to the successful implementations of DPM.

We are grateful to Tony Attard, CEO and founder of Panaz, who supported the idea that Panaz would be the test case for our new *Dynamic Portfolio Management* module.[9] Tony also graciously agreed to let us use his name as well as that of the Panaz company.

We are especially grateful to Mike Gibbins, Panaz's Head of Supply Chain, Quality, and New Product Development, for allowing us to publish the interview presented in Chapter 6. Mike's candid assessment of the positive impact of DPM on Panaz is a significant and valuable contribution to the book.

We would like to thank Ged Leigh for his invaluable contribution to the success of the Panaz project. Ged delivered the follow-on, in-company coaching sessions, which reinforced the prioritization of products and the scoring model, and firmly embedded the DPM concepts at Panaz.

Stephen Kay would like to thank the dozen or so associates who delivered the ASAM materials to a wide range of companies and learners. Their commitment, professionalism and dedication helped make the ASAM program such a success.

Roger Warburton would like to thank Boston University's Metropolitan College for the 2017 *Chadwick Award* for faculty development. The *Chadwick Award* paid for

[9] Panaz is no ordinary company. In 2014, Panaz was included in the *Financial Times Stock Exchange* list of top 1,000 companies to inspire Britain.

travel to the U.K. to interview companies about their experiences with *Dynamic Portfolio Management*. In particular, the interview with Mike Gibbins in Chapter 6 was supported by the *Chadwick Award*.

We are grateful to Eileen Warburton, who copy-edited the book. Without her skills, there would be random commas and peculiar wording throughout. Of course, all mistakes remain our responsibility.

INTRODUCTION

Which new products should a company invest in?

New products often account for over 50% of a company's growth and 40% of their profits. [1] Therefore, it is not much of an exaggeration to say that a company's future depends on the success rate of its new products. Selecting the products to invest in requires predicting which of them will be successful.[10]

Therefore, while difficult, businesses are obliged to attempt to predict the future. That is, which of their new products will return the best investment?

Many companies struggle with this question and, if the research is to be believed, most are not very good at answering it. In fact, only one out of four product development projects succeeds commercially, one-third of all new product launches flop, and over 45% of development resources are wasted on ventures that fail. [1]

If it is so important, why are companies so bad at it?

Many companies have a mix of products under development, including innovative developments, modest extensions of successful lines, technology investments, legally mandated compliance projects, and strategic corporate initiatives. In such a complex, dynamic environment, how does a company prioritize and pursue an appropriate mix of projects?

Symptoms of Poor Portfolio Management

One of the most common symptoms of weak portfolio management is a reluctance to kill off poorly performing products, which results in too many projects competing for too few resources. Once approved, projects acquire a life of their own and often continue without critical technical reviews, without project management assessment of progress, without customer feedback, and without market feasibility assessments.

The lack of a formal process for evaluating products results in companies missing positive opportunities for significant product improvements. They fail to take ad-

[10] Niels Bohr, the Nobel Prize winning physicist, famously said that "prediction is very difficult, especially about the future."

vantage of evolving marketing information and evaluations of early test versions by customers. Poor portfolio management can also result in investment in products that don't support the corporate strategy.

The overall result is that companies tend to release too many mediocre products and too few genuinely successful winners.

Product Portfolio Management

On the other hand, a few companies do actually excel at introducing new products and *Fortune's* list of the most admired companies contains some of the most innovative firms: 3M, Intel, Guinness, General Electric, Johnson & Johnson, Procter & Gamble, and others.

What can be learned from these successful companies? One of the most important observations is that successful products provide customers with unique and valuable benefits and the success rate for such products can exceed 80%.

If greater success in new product development can, in fact, be achieved, it should be possible to educate companies in the successful methods that lead to improvements.[11] And, indeed, the current research proposes methods and techniques that are validated, successful, and surprisingly straightforward. Once the critical success factors are understood, business processes can be implemented that are both easy-to-understand and effective.[12]

The process of selecting the right portfolio of products is called Product Portfolio Management (PPM). This book presents a modern, state-of-the-art approach to PPM.

Dynamic Portfolio Management

Recent research has shown that company portfolios are dynamic and that the traditional, static methods of PPM need to be upgraded to accommodate evolution and change in the portfolio from both internal and external factors. [2] Internally, the portfolio must react to evolving customer demands, differing rates of project progress, and revised marketing priorities. The external business environment is also dynamic and the portfolio must react to strategic company initiatives, market changes, and technological and social forces.

Projects are often started with a universal expectation of success, even for risky, high technology ventures. As development proceeds, a prototype is delivered, marketing data becomes available, and an evolved picture of the product emerges: maybe the product performs differently from what was envisioned, the market

[11] Cooper's *Winning at New Products* presents these issues in a clear and readable way.

[12] Cooper suggests that the processes "fit management's way of working," which is a polite way of saying they are simple enough for even management to understand.

might be different than anticipated, and unforeseen risks may have occurred. This dynamism in content operates in addition to the classic project management issues of changing costs and schedules.

This new information requires a re-assessments of the technical and marketing position of the product as well as its strategic contribution to the portfolio. Therefore, dynamic processes are required to support changes in technical content, to adapt to evolving markets, and generally to evolve the portfolio consistent with corporate strategy.

The central topic of the book is the *Bargery Fabrics Case*, which fills the need for a case that teaches students in classes and learners in companies the modern techniques of *Dynamic Portfolio Management*. By working through the *Bargery Fabrics Case* students learn how to evaluate a portfolio, how to select which products the company should invest in, and how to ensure that their selected portfolio matches the strategic goals of their company. The students work through exercises in stages, with each stage consisting of a mini-lecture, a case exercise, questions, and discussion materials.

The *Bargery Fabrics Case* first walks students through a fairly traditional approach to Product Portfolio Management (PPM), which is founded on Cooper's extensive research that has established a successful track record. [1] The case then takes the students through *Dynamic Portfolio Management*, which adds the latest techniques in the dynamic aspects of portfolio management to the *Bargery Fabrics Case*.

Contents

Chapter 1 presents the *Bargery Fabrics* company. The company is in transition and requires help in *Dynamic Portfolio Management*.

Bargery Fabrics specializes in the manufacture of innovative fabrics in the medical and health care markets. While the company is successful, many of their products are maturing. The new CEO has proposed that the company develop a new product portfolio.

Chapter 2 presents the products under development at *Bargery Fabrics*.

Chapter 3 presents a market study, which estimates the future potential of the various market sectors in which *Bargery Fabrics* competes. The chapter also describes the development status of each of the products, along with the estimated funds required to complete each project.

Chapter 4 presents a list of assignments to be worked through. There are five sequential assignments that allow the reader to develop their own solution gradually in understandable stages. The assignments guide the reader through the steps necessary to create, analyze, and defend a portfolio.

Chapter 5 presents detailed, worked solutions for the assignments. Since there is no single, one-size-fits-all solution, we provide alternative answers and suggestions. Each solution is followed by guidance for conducting the case as well as discussion questions along with suggested approaches. The chapter concludes with a discussion about the general issues that often arise when running the case.

Chapter 6 presents the results of running of the case in real-world companies. The highlight is the description of the implementation of *Dynamic Portfolio Management* at Panaz.

Chapter 7 presents a *Teaching Note*, which includes sample learning outcomes and explains why the case's goals for students and company learners are realistic. The *Teaching Note* also discusses the issues, misunderstandings, and mistakes that often arise.

The *Teaching Note* presents teaching strategies for the two proposed audiences: graduate students in classes and learners in companies. While the audiences are different, the *Bargery Fabrics Case* is used unchanged. Teaching plans are provided, along with a discussion of the relatively minor differences in approach necessitated by the different audiences. A sample exam question, and notional solution, is provided for classroom usage.

Chapter 8 discusses the *Research* that forms the foundation for the book. We summarize the essential topics, provide an annotated guide to the relevant literature, and list suggested topics for instructors to include in a presentation of the materials before tackling the case.

Side Notes and Citations

This is the *Instructor's Document* and is annotated with side notes that immediately highlight important issues in context.[13]

Side notes are numbered sequentially through each chapter. The notes appear on the same page as the number.[14]

[13]This is a side note, which illustrates side notes.

[14]Side notes fall towards the bottom of the same page as the number.

Side notes help instructors by pointing out immediately relevant contextual information, such as the applicable theoretical concept, a critical piece of data, or relevant technical information. As instructors read through the case, side notes highlight the subtleties and significance of relevant information. Also, when students overlook specific, key information about *Bargery Fabrics*, or struggle to support their arguments with data, the side notes help the instructor to identify quickly the relevant information.

Formal citations of other works are given in brackets, e.g., for a book on Project Management, see [3]. The references are collected in the *Bibliography* at the end of the book.

There is only one index, because we think that looking up concepts and authors separately is confusing. In this book everything and everyone is in the single index. Neither is there a separate glossary, as that duplicates information. Terms are defined in their context and indexed.

A student and learners' version of the *Bargery Fabrics Case* is also available. It contains the chapters that cover the *Bargery Fabrics* case, the description of the products, the marketing and financial status, and the assignments, i.e., Chapters 1 through 4. The learners' version does not include side notes. These materials can be provided to students and company learners to prepare for running the case.

Cases

Cases develop student skills in problem solving, the use of analysis tools, quantitative reasoning, and decision making in complex situations. One of the more valuable features of cases is that they teach students to deal with the types of ambiguities they face in their careers and to develop solutions to open-ended problems with multiple potential solutions.

This case includes a teaching note, which identifies the important learning objectives, explains its usefulness and relevance, defines audience expectations, and outlines a teaching plan. For the instructor, the teaching note includes advice on how to manage discussion sessions, gives feedback about previous iterations of the case, and provides guidance on typical misunderstandings and mistakes made by the students.

Unlike lectures, cases do not follow a script and instructors must learn to guide students toward their own solutions. In that context, instructors face a number of challenges, including learning what information in the case is relevant to which theoretical concepts. Here, we provide side notes to guide the instructor through these issues.

SYNOPSIS

A Dynamic Portfolio for *Bargery Fabrics*

Bargery Fabrics

William Bargery, known to everyone as "Old Bill," has decided to retire as President of *Bargery Fabrics*, but he is reluctant to hand over the reins to his son, Mark, because they are in conflict about the future direction of the company.

Bargery Fabrics is a well-established manufacturer of innovative fabrics. They specialize in adding antimicrobial agents to fabrics, which slows the growth of bacteria, mold, and fungi, and eliminates odors. They compete in the medical and health care markets, selling to hospitals, nursing homes, and the public.

William Bargery believes that his company's success in the demanding health care market is attributable to their technical prowess and their rapid response to customer requests. Mark Bargery, who is reluctant to challenge his father, believes that their technical achievements, while impressive, are insufficient.

Mark recently conducted a review of the entire company and the outward signs are positive: *Bargery Fabrics* is growing and profitable. However, many of their products are maturing and experiencing increased competition. Mark also discovered that *Bargery Fabrics* has neither a strategy for future product investment nor processes to select which of their proposed products are most likely to succeed commercially.

Therefore, Mark Bargery proposed a new strategy: *Bargery Fabrics* should invest in a revitalized, innovative product portfolio oriented towards the medical and health care markets, where they have a competitive advantage. They should also develop a portfolio management system that determines their products' critical success factors, allocates research funds wisely, produces a roadmap for development, and ensures their products implement the new business strategy.

To convince his father, Mark needs a detailed plan that defends his strategy.

Motivation for the *Bargery Fabrics Case*

Which of their new products should a company invest in?

Many companies struggle with this question and, if the research is to be believed, most are not very good at it. On the other hand, new products often account for over 50% of a company's growth and 40% of their profits. Therefore, a company's future may depend prominently on the success of its new products.

Unfortunately, many companies are bad at it.

Fortunately, current research suggests that, with suitable education and training, the answer is surprisingly straightforward: *Dynamic Portfolio Management*, which is both effective and easy-to-understand.

Research has established that modern portfolios are dynamic. Products in the portfolio must adapt to changes, such as evolving customer demands and different rates of technical progress. The external business environment is also dynamic, which requires that the portfolio implements the company's strategy, responds to market changes, and adapts to technological and social forces.

Companies regard portfolio management as a competitive weapon and are, therefore, understandably reluctant to publish their data and to share their strategy. As a result, there are few workable cases in portfolio management.

Audience, Skills, and Learning Outcomes

There are two target audiences for the case: learners in a traditional company setting and students in graduate management courses. The approach in companies, which takes a day to complete, is to alternate brief seminars with workshops in which the assignments are completed. In management classes, students are prepared in lectures and the case can then be completed in a single three-hour session.

The *Bargery Fabrics Case* is designed to help students master the critical success factors underlying a successful portfolio; the evaluation of products with realistic characteristics; the key portfolio evaluation tools, such as the product selection matrix and the roadmap; the allocation of the budget; the assessment of the dynamic aspects of the portfolio; and the development and presentation of a coherent new product strategy.

The case includes worked assignments with multiple solutions, discussion questions, lessons from real companies, a teaching note with learning outcomes and teaching plans, and an annotated summary of the relevant research.

1

BARGERY FABRICS

1.1 Background

William Bargery, known to everyone as "Old Bill," has decided to retire as President of Bargery Fabrics. William Bargery earned a degree in Chemical Engineering and, working for his father who founded the company, invented fast, cost-effective processes for applying specialized coatings to fabrics that provided their customers with unique, innovative products. *Bargery Fabrics* is well-established and has an excellent reputation in the health care market. They sell to hospitals, private nursing homes, and directly to the public.

Lately, William's son, Mark, following in his father's footsteps, developed successful new product lines. By adding antimicrobial agents to fibers, Mark created fabrics that slow the growth of microorganisms, bacteria, mold, and fungi, and eliminate odors in clothing and shoes.[1]

While William Bargery lauds his son's technical achievements, he is reluctant to hand over the reins because they are in conflict about the future direction of the company. William Bargery believes that his company's success in the demanding health care market, where customers have challenging product requirements, is directly attributable to their innovation, their technical prowess, and their ability to tailor their products rapidly to their customers' demands.

Mark Bargery, who is reluctant to challenge his father directly, believes that prod-

[1] The first essential theme: The company can create unique, valuable products, see Critical Success Factors.

1

uct success requires far more. Unlike his father, Mark Bargery believes that technical achievements are not sufficient and that the company can no longer rely on just responding to their customer's requests, they need to define a coherent product strategy.

Mark Bargery conducted a thorough review of the state of the entire company and the outward signs are positive: *Bargery Fabrics* is growing and profitable. However, while many of their products are currently successful, they are maturing and experiencing increasing competition.[2] A particularly worrying conclusion from his study was that *Bargery Fabrics* has neither a strategy for future product investment nor processes to select which of their proposed products are most likely to succeed commercially.[3]

Mark also understands that the *Bargery Fabrics* staff has always done things a particular way and are loyal to Old Bill. He knows he will have to tread carefully.[4]

Bargery Fabrics has annual sales of $30 million and employs some 200 people.

1.2 A New Product Portfolio

Mark understands that *Bargery Fabrics* is successful at manufacturing technically sophisticated medical and health care products.[5] However, his study revealed that *Bargery Fabrics* tries to respond to all customer requests and, as a result, have many products under development that have limited commercial potential. Old Bill's mantra is that they need to keep their customers happy.[6]

Mark believes that the company cannot continue with their unfocused approach and that, while they must maintain their technical prowess, they must also develop new products that can compete in attractive markets.[7]

Therefore, Mark recently proposed a new business strategy for *Bargery Fabrics:*

- Invest in a revitalized, innovative new product portfolio oriented towards the medical and health care markets, where their products should have a competitive advantage and where they have an established market presence.

- Develop a new system for managing their portfolio: determine the critical success factors for their products, allocate development funds wisely, produce a roadmap for future development, and ensure the proposed portfolio implements the new business strategy.

[2]The maturing products theme: *Bargery Fabrics* needs new, innovative products.

[3]Another essential theme: A lack of business processes to select which products are likely to be successful.

[4]New product development is a collaborative, multi-department process. It empowers lower level staff members, whose decisions must be respected.

[5]Reinforcing the theme that *Bargery Fabrics'* successful products are in specific markets: medical and health care.

[6]Many companies have too many products under development, which results in the release of mediocre products.

[7]See the definition of an attractive market and *Blue Ocean Strategy.*

Old Bill is skeptical and Mark understands that, if he is to succeed his father, his strategy must be convincing.[8]

1.3 Mark Bargery's New Strategy

Bargery Fabrics manufactures a wide range of products, including: wound care items (band aids, bandages, and orthopedic padding); protective apparel (masks, gowns, and uniforms); anti-microbial sportswear, furnishings and bedding; shoe and garment linings; and advanced high-performance garments with thermal and fire protection.[9]

Bargery Fabrics' products are developed in-house by a small, but capable, staff of versatile laboratory chemists who treat fibers with specialized finishes to produce fabrics that perform better than off-the-shelf materials and, often, are tailored to meet specific customers' requirements.[10]

Mark Bargery began by acknowledging that *Bargery Fabrics* has been successful in the medical and health care markets where customers have demanding requirements and detailed specifications. However, Mark's marketing study showed that several of *Bargery Fabrics'* successful products are maturing and coming under increasing competitive threats, both from European imports and from large companies in the USA. Competitors are beginning to add anti-microbial and anti-odor features to their low-cost, commodity products, which is increasing the competition at the low end of the market.[11]

One of the challenges of medical and health care products is that they are subject to many regulations and must undergo extensive user trials to establish their safety.[12] While this lengthens the development cycle, it also creates a high barrier to entry for competitors.[13]

Mark Bargery believes that *Bargery Fabrics* can flourish in the medical and health care business sectors because they understand the market and already have a number of successful products there. In particular, the company has a significant, growing presence in the market for more innovative products, such as orthopedic padding and surgical wound dressings.[14] On the other hand, Mark predicts that their commodity products will become less successful due to the increased pressure for lower prices.[15]

Mark Bargery's marketing study concluded that the medical and health care sectors are large and extremely diverse. Therefore, in order to succeed, Mark proposed that *Bargery Fabrics* would need a clear, market-focused strategy. Mark is confident that there is are significant opportunities in the medical and health care

---

[8]See Assignment #5: Present your proposed portfolio to upper management.

[9]If this sounds like a lot of products, it is; they need to prune their product list.

[10]Developing high quality products to meet specific customer demands generates unique products.

[11]This will make it difficult for *Bargery Fabrics* to compete against giant companies in the low-cost, commodity markets.

[12]The completion of user trials is important since it is when products start generating sales and income.

[13]A high barrier to entry discourages competitors, which makes for an attractive market.

[14]These products are innovative and, therefore, *unique and differentiated*—the most important critical success factor.

[15]For "commodity" products, many are alike and, so, the market is price sensitive—a red ocean.

3

markets because they are attractive and growing.[16] However, to compete, *Bargery fabrics* will have to make major investments in new products, management processes, staff, and laboratory facilities.

Mark Bargery summarized his conclusions as follows:

- While *Bargery Fabrics'* products have been very successful, many are becoming mature and are suffering from price competition.[17]

- *Bargery Fabrics* does not have a process for selecting which products to pursue nor for evaluating the progress of projects under development.[18] Neither do they have clear criteria for accepting nor rejecting new projects.[19]

- There are far too many small projects underway, many with little potential return. Projects are often incremental in nature and involve developing specific fabrics for established customers.

- Although failure rates for new ventures are high, there is great reluctance to kill off projects once they are started.[20]

As a result, Mark Bargery has proposed a new strategy for *Bargery Fabrics:*

- Increase *Bargery Fabrics'* capabilities in medical and health care products. Since they currently sell to hospitals and private nursing homes, they understand the market.[21]

    - They are well-established in the business space and there is a high barrier to entry for competitors.[22]

    - They have the required resources, technical expertise, and customer knowledge to develop demanding health care products.[23]

- Instead of devoting resources to many, small projects and maturing product lines, *Bargery Fabrics* should invest in more innovative products with long-term payoff.

- Long-term product development must be balanced with products that can be brought to market quickly to generate sales.[24]

- Focus on innovative products.

    - Replace or refresh the increasingly mature commodities in the portfolio with new, unique, innovative products.

[16]See the market study, section 3.1.

[17]*Bargery Fabrics* will need to move away from maturing products in competitive, commodity markets.

[18]This emphasizes the need for a new portfolio management system.

[19]The *Critical Success Factors* are the key to product selection.

[20]This is a common problem—companies are reluctant to "kill the dogs."

[21]A focused marketing strategy.

[22]They can create unique products in attractive markets.

[23]The strategy is feasible.

[24]This will become a major feature of the roadmap: selecting products that can generate early sales.

– Introduce innovative, new products into attractive markets.

Mark Bargery has proposed to allocate increased funding for the development of new, innovative products where *Bargery Fabrics'* skills and capabilities should prove to be a unique and powerful combination. Mark has allocated a budget of $600,000 for next year's new product developments.[25]

To convince his father, Mark needs to develop a detailed plan that defends his new company strategy.[26]

[25]The budget will become important after the products have been scored in the *selection matrix*.

[26]This is sets up a continuing theme for the assignments: proposing and defending the presentation of the strategy at each stage of the process.

2

BARGERY FABRICS' PRODUCTS

Bargery Fabrics has a number of new products under development. Each product competes in a specific market and makes use of one or more technology platforms.[1] The proposed products are grouped into the following market areas:

1. Dressings and wound care.

2. Protective and hygiene apparel.

3. Hygienic bedding and furnishing materials.

4. Miscellaneous products.

2.1 Dressings and wound care

2.1.1 #1: First aid dressings

These are band aids and dressings primarily for consumer use. This is a high-volume, mature, and price-sensitive market, with many well-established companies.[2] *Bargery Fabrics* already has products in this market, but is seeking to develop new products that contain anti-microbial treatments.

Because of price considerations, *Bargery Fabrics* is investigating the use of bio-active fiber coatings to create innovative products that could differentiate them

[1] The strategy is more cost-effective when multiple products use the same underlying technology platform and when multiple products are sold in the same market.

[2] The key words here are "mature" and "price sensitive." These types of products are less attractive to *Bargery Fabrics*. They wish to steer away from competing against large companies with low-cost products.

from the competition. These new bio-active coatings are based on naturally occurring compounds, such as chitosan, which is a fiber derived from the hard outer shells of crustaceans such as crabs, crayfish, and shrimp.

Chitosan is abundant, exhibits antimicrobial activity, and is biodegradable. Coatings made from chitosan are not allergenic, which makes them safe for biomedical and health care applications.

The technology platform is called "bio-active coatings."

2.1.2 #2: Orthopedic padding

These products provide extra padding and protection under plaster casts and in shoes. *Bargery Fabrics* already supplies substantial volumes to other companies who market the end products. However, *Bargery Fabrics* sees more sales potential and growth if they package the products themselves and re-target them for use in hospitals and nursing homes.[3]

The anti-microbial and, more particularly, anti-fungal properties of these products are more demanding than for first-aid dressings. Odor prevention over a period of several weeks is also highly desirable.

Two technology platforms are appropriate:

1. The blending of small quantities of copper-coated fibers into the fabrics, which results in fabrics that are relatively expensive, but careful control of the blending process may reduce costs. The technology platform is called "metalized fibers."

2. An alternative is the combination of anti-fungal agents along with essential aromatherapy oils in slow release capsules. This is a smaller and more specialized market.[4] The technology platform is called "micro encapsulation."

2.1.3 #3: Wound dressings

This is a medical market where *Bargery Fabrics* already has a significant presence and their products are sold for surgical and clinical use. *Bargery Fabrics* regards this as one of their most critical products and believe that it will provide the greatest opportunities for in-house development, packaging, and direct sale to end users, especially in the health care sector.[5]

The most appropriate anti-microbial agent is metallic silver, which can be incorporated into fabrics in several forms. Extensive and costly clinical trials are neces-

[3]Low technical risk, but some risks associated with marketing the products themselves.

[4]And, therefore, not a particularly *attractive market.*

[5]This is important information. *Bargery Fabrics* believes that wound dressings are their most important potential product. The CSFs and the scoring matrix should reflect this. An important question for the strategy discussion is: How have the students included the idea that *Bargery Fabrics* believes wound dressings are important?

8

sary to certify and market these products. The technology platform is "metalized fibers."

2.2 Protective Apparel

2.2.1 #4: Gowns and Drapes

Bargery Fabrics does not, as yet, have an established presence in the gowns and drapes market, but has conducted preliminary market studies.[6] *Bargery Fabrics* is in negotiations to license a proven coating technology that they can apply to one of their fabrics.[7] Sales volumes are potentially large, but royalty costs are also likely to be high, reducing the profit margins.[8]

Also, *Bargery Fabrics* would be bound into a restrictive agreement and would not be able to enhance the technology.[9] There are also significant risks: the emergence of alternative and improved technologies and superior (or cheaper) products may appear on the market.[10]

The technology platform is proprietary and classified under "miscellaneous."

2.2.2 #5: Face Masks

Bargery Fabrics already produces filtration fabrics for face masks. This is a high volume, low cost, and highly competitive market that is dominated by large global companies.[11]

The application of cheap metalized fibers could produce an innovative product that could compete in the market place.

2.2.3 #6: Replaceable Insoles

Odor control in boot and shoe insoles is a large, existing market for *Bargery Fabrics* and there is considerable scope for improved fabric technology. *Bargery Fabrics'* current line is based on odor-eating particulates, but an enhanced anti-microbial fabric containing metalized fibers is close to commercialization.[12]

Most shoes are now manufactured offshore and the market is for low cost products for export.[13]

2.2.4 #7: Sports and Leisurewear

Bargery Fabrics is considering developing a range of anti-microbial fabrics for the sports and leisure industries based on silver and copper metalized fibers technol-

[6] Preliminary data, so market risk

[7] This is a *licensed* product, which means *Bargery Fabrics* does not control the technology. Can they create a unique product?

[8] High potential sales vs. lower profitability.

[9] This product often turns out to be one of the borderline selections. The debate will center around high sales vs. low profit margins and, because of licensing restrictions, that they have little control over the product.

[10] The appearance of competitive products will mean less uniqueness and lower the product's long-term attractiveness.

[11] Immediately making it a very unattractive market.

[12] The only characteristic making this product attractive is that it is close to commercialization, which makes this a candidate for inclusion in the portfolio if short term sales are required.

[13] An unattractive, low-cost market.

ogy. *Bargery Fabrics* is also considering developing odor-eating fabrics based on micro-encapsulation technology. Neither development project has yet started.[14]

Offshore garment production is likely to account for a high proportion of the demand.[15]

2.2.5 #8: Protective Garments

Bargery Fabrics is working on developing high-end protective garments, such as fireman's clothing. These are highly technical products, requiring multiple advanced fabrics that provide unique characteristics,[16] including a protective outer layer (Kevlar, Nomex, etc.), a middle layer of anti-microbial technology, and an inner layer for comfort offering a breathable, moisture barrier (micro-porous Gortex etc.).[17]

These will be manufactured locally in cooperation with *Bargery Fabrics*.

The ability to combine one or more anti-microbial technology platforms (metalized fibers, odor-eating micro-encapsulation and re-chargeable coatings) with specialized fabrics is likely to be required in order to achieve the high levels of performance.[18]

2.3 Hygienic Bedding and Furnishing Materials

2.3.1 #9: Hospital Bedding

The introduction of metalized fibers into hospital bedding and furnishing liners can provide protection against hospital-borne infections, which is a growing concern. This is an example of the "metalized fibers" technology platform.

In a hospital, bedding is laundered regularly in dedicated facilities. In such an environment, the application of rechargeable anti-microbial finishes on the fabric is a valuable asset if it can be carefully controlled.[19]

This is an example of the "rechargeable coatings" technology platform.

2.3.2 # 10: Domestic Bedding

A major problem encountered in the domestic bedding and furnishing market is dust mite allergies. *Bargery Fabrics* is planning to develop advanced fabrics for mattress covers by buying closely woven micro-fiber fabrics and adding specially-developed, custom-treated linings.

[14]Note: They are "considering" it, which means they have little information and that there could be significant risks.

[15]Off-shore manufacturing suggests that the products are likely to be cost sensitive and, therefore, an unattractive market.

[16]Note: *unique*.

[17]All of this establishes the product as unique and differentiated.

[18] A key strength of *Bargery Fabrics* is their ability to work with customers to produce fabrics with specific properties and to tailor the fabrics to meet demanding regulations, i.e, making unique products.

[19]A key strength for *Bargery Fabrics* is the ability to work with customers to produce innovative fabrics tailored to satisfy demanding requirements.

10

Bargery Fabrics will also look at purchasing a range of fabrics for sheets and pillow-cases to complement this product line. Initially, anti-microbial metalized fibers will be incorporated into the fabric. However, metalized fibers only have a limited effective lifetime against repeated washing, so *Bargery Fabrics* intends to start research into the re-chargeable coatings technology platform.

2.4 Miscellaneous Products

2.4.1 #11: Smart Materials

Bargery Fabrics is collaborating with a local university to develop "smart wearable fabrics." This is a research project with the goal of developing fabrics that automatically indicate what is going on under a dressing, e.g., the fabric would change color to indicate the spread of an infection or the discharge of fluid. These technologies are still at an early stage of development and may be three years away from commercialization.

The technology platform is classified under "miscellaneous."

2.4.2 #12: Silver Monitoring

The increase in the commercial use of silver in fabrics, along with concerns about its impact on the environment, has led the government to require companies to monitor and report their consumption of silver. *Bargery Fabrics* has proposed that their Information Technology (IT) department develop and test an automated information system for tracking and monitoring their use of silver.[20]

The technology platform is classified under "miscellaneous."

2.5 Technology Platforms

Most existing anti-microbial fabrics contain synthetic organic compounds. However, it is expected that, in the long-term, there will be a move away from these chemical anti-microbial finishes. Concern about many conventional chemical finishes and their impact on the environment, as well as on users, means that there is a growing level of interest in newer anti-microbial technologies. New government regulations will have a significant, long-term impact on the market.

As a result, the following new anti-microbial technology platforms are of interest.

[20]Note that this is a "Compliance Project." It is included, despite the fact that it has no market potential.

2.5.1 Bio-Active Coatings

An interesting new technology is the use of naturally occurring fibers, such as chitosan, which demonstrates natural anti-microbial properties. Chitosan fibers can be blended into fabrics.

There is growing interest in such materials for health care and medical applications. At present, however, the technology is probably better suited to the good-living end of the market spectrum rather than for surgical and clinical uses.[21]

2.5.2 Metalized Fibers

Over the past several years, there has been growing interest in the use of silver (and, to a more limited extent, copper) for medical and high-performance anti-microbial applications. There are several ways of introducing the silver into the fabrics but all are relatively expensive.

Copper-based fibers are widely used as a lower cost alternative to silver, but not necessarily in the most critical medical or health care applications. Copper is well suited to anti-fungal applications.

2.5.3 Micro-Encapsulation

Controlled release of active agents from micro-encapsulated finishes on fabrics is already a proven technology and improvements are likely to emerge quickly. At present, this technique is successfully and widely employed for fragrances and natural aromatherapy oils. *Bargery Fabrics* plans to develop the technology for critical medical applications.[22]

2.5.4 Rechargeable Coatings

The effectiveness of anti-microbial technologies tends to decline after many washings of the fabric. However, a relatively simple chlorine wash can recharge the anti-microbial effectiveness. The technology already exists and is available via license.[23] The rechargeable coatings technology may have considerable potential in protective clothing applications, where textile rental, cleaning, and maintenance companies operate.

Table 2.1 summarizes the relation between the proposed products and their associated technology platforms.

[21] While an attractive long-term option, the technology is speculative and risky for *Bargery Fabrics*' desired applications in health care.

[22] This is a new, untried technology and, therefore, more risky.

[23] Licensing is less attractive financially and the company would have less control over the technology.

12

Table 2.1: New products and their technology platforms.

		Bio Active Coatings	Metalized Fibers	Micro En-capsulation	Recharge-able Coats	Miscell-aneous
1	First Aid Dressings	■				
2	Orthopedic Padding		■	■		
3 5	Wound Dressings		■			
4	Gowns & Drapes					■
5	Face Masks		■			
6	Replaceable Insoles		■			
7	Sports & Leisurewear		■	■		
8	Protective Garments		■	■	■	■
9	Hospital Bedding		■		■	
10	Domestic Bedding		■		■	
11	Smart Materials					■
12	Silver Monitoring					■

13

3

MARKET DATA AND PROJECT STATUS

3.1 Market Data

Bargery Fabrics employed a consulting company to conduct a survey of the future potential of the antimicrobial market sectors. The resulting report provided data on potential market sizes.

Bargery Fabrics is interested in the following four market segments:

- *Bio Active Coatings:*

  This includes medical wound dressings and the market is growing rapidly; it is currently projected to grow at around 15% per year.

- *Metalized Fibers:*

  This is a diverse market that includes lingerie and underwear, sport and leisurewear, and bedding.[1]

- *Micro-encapsulation:*

  There is an established market in fragrances, but the application to health care is new. Products include hospital uniforms, drapes, face masks, and shoes.

[1] Notice that the potential bedding volumes in Table 3.1 are very large, making it an attractive market.

15

- *Re-Chargeable Coatings:*

   This is a new market with an uncertain demand. Products include hospital furnishings and bedding.

The estimated potential market size for each of the segments is presented in Table 3.1. The table lists the potential sales contribution of anti-microbial fabrics (not the sales volume of the products) in tons per annum (tpa).[2]

Table 3.1: Potential Market Volumes.

Market Segment	Products	Volume (tpa)
1) Bio Active Coatings	Medical wound dressings	5,500
2) Metalized fibers	Hosiery (socks & tights)	13,000
	Lingerie & underwear	5,000
	Men's underwear	1,000
	Sportswear	15,000
	Leisurewear	7,000
	Bedding:	
	—Mattress covers	50,000
	—Duvets & quilts	15,000
	—Fibers, wadding	12,000
	—Blankets	2,000
3) Micro-encapsulation	Health care, nurse uniforms	4,000
	Drapes	6,000
	Food industry	5,000
	Face masks	2,000
	Shoes, linings	6,000
4) Re-Chargeable Coatings	Hospital furnishings	6,000
	Hospital bedding	4,000

3.2 Project Status

Table 3.2 presents the status of each of the projects in the portfolio. The table lists the project's progress, estimated completion dates, and the estimated budget to complete the project.

[2]While market data is important, it must be used with caution as it is a guess about the future.

16

Table 3.2: Project Status and Financial Estimates.

Project	Status
1) First Aid Dressings	Well underway. Initial samples with customers have shown good results. To complete: $75K, 6 months.
2) Orthopedic Padding	Almost ready: Few technological problems anticipated for Copper technology. User trials, 6 months. Micro-encapsulation development, 12 months. To complete: $150K.
3) Wound Dressings	Basic development completed and products could be on the market within 3 months. Continuing expenditures are anticipated in order to adapt to new markets. To complete: $170K/year for 3-5 years.
4) Gowns & Drapes	Licensed technology almost ready for immediate commercialization. Thereafter, relatively high royalty costs. To complete: $50K, 6 months.
5) Face Masks	Technology proven. Tests required for user acceptance. To complete: 2 years at $200K per year.
6) Replaceable Insoles	Technology proven. Commercialization within 6 months. Consumer promotion required thereafter. To complete: $85K, 6 months.
7) Sports & Leisurewear	Not started, but synergies from metalized fibers technology being transferred from medical products. 2 years to complete the initial product. Continuing development to support customization of products. To complete: $150K/year for 2 years.
8) Protective Garments	Not started but synergies from other technologies. Continuing product development support to customers thereafter at $200K/year. To complete: $180K, 18 months + 6 months user trials.
9) Hospital Bedding	Major uncertainties about hospital procurement regulations, requirements and priorities 3-5 years ahead. To complete: $120K, 12 months + 1 year user trials.
10) Domestic Bedding	Basic development already underway. To complete: $120K, 1 year.

Continued on next page

17

Project	Status
11) Smart Materials	Collaboration with University. Relatively small investment, but will require a more substantial development over the next 3 years: $500K in all, if proven. To complete: $90K, 1 year feasibility study.
12) Silver Monitoring	Government mandated data collection system. Project has not started. To complete: $50K, 5 months to build, 1 month test.

CHAPTER

ASSIGNMENTS

This chapter lists the assignments for readers to work through. They are presented here without answers so that readers may attempt their own solutions. Completing the assignments in order will guide the reader through the steps necessary to create a portfolio.

4.1 Assignment #1

From the *Bargery Fabrics* strategy, complete the first two rows of the *Selection Matrix:* The Selection Criteria and the Weights.

4.2 Assignment #2

Complete the portfolio *Selection Matrix*.

For all products, assign a score to each selection criterion and calculate its total score.

4.3 Assignment #3

Allocate the budget to the top products.

Sort the *Selection Matrix* so that the products with the highest scores are at the top. Allocate funds until the product development budget of $600,000 is consumed.

4.4 Assignment #4

Recommend a product strategy for *Bargery Fabrics*.

4.5 Assignment #5

Assess the portfolio and develop a *roadmap*.

Present the portfolio to upper management and defend your rationale.

CHAPTER **5**

ASSIGNMENT ANSWERS

5.1   Assignment #1

From the Bargery Fabrics strategy, complete the first two rows of the Selection Matrix: The Selection Criteria and the Weights.

5.1.1   Solution for Assignment #1

The first step ion the development of a portfolio of new products is to formulate a clear statement of the company strategy. Mark Bargery clearly lays out the strategy for *Bargery Fabrics* in section 1.3.

Students and learners should develop a suitable list of selection criteria (no more than 5 or 6) for *Bargery Fabrics*. Their criteria should be firmly based on the Critical Success Factors (CSFs) and tailored to *Bargery Fabrics'* strategy.

They should carefully define what each of their own criteria and weights mean. They should be able to explain precisely why they are using those criteria and how they intend to score them.[1]

Next, a weight is assigned to each criterion with a value from 0-5, where 5 means the criterion is of the highest importance. A sample definition of the importance of the weights is shown in Table 5.1.

[1] Students have a tendency to discuss things in great detail without taking notes. Later, when they come to score the criteria, they forget what led them to establish those criteria and why they thought them important. Therefore, students should be encouraged to document their rationale.

Table 5.1: Defining the value of the Weights.

Selection Criteria	Weight
The future of *Bargery Fabrics* depends on it	5
Very important aspect of their strategic goals	4
Important	3
Not very important	2
Small impact	1
No impact	0

Students should be encouraged to document their rationale and a sample might look like Table 5.2. The *Rationale* column explains why the criteria were selected and why the weights have the values they do.[2]

Table 5.2: Documenting the Rationale for the Selection Criteria and Weights.

Selection Criteria	Weight	Rationale
Unique, differentiated product	5	Research establishes this as the most important CSF.
Financially Attractive	2	Lower weight because less important CSF and difficult to predict financial data.
Strategic Fit	3	Advantageous when common technology platforms & marketing. Conforms to company strategy.

The end result is the completion of the first two rows of the *selection matrix* and one possible solution is shown in Table 5.3.

Table 5.3: Assignment #1: Solution for Selection Criteria and Weights.

Selection Criteria	Unique Differentiated	Attractive Market	Capacity, Technical Feasibility	Financial Attractiveness	Strategic Fit
Weight	5	4	3	2	3

The criteria and their weights should be documented and examples are as follows.

- *Unique, Differentiated Product (Weight = 5):*

[2]Students can be reminded that they will have to explain their criteria and weights to the other teams.

22

This has been shown to be the most important factor in determining the success of a product. Therefore, the weight for this criterion should be the maximum, which is 5.

To achieve a high score, the product must provide real benefits and value to the customer, be a unique, quality product, and have positive, valuable attributes that are easily perceived by the customer.

It is important to note that both "unique" and "differentiated" are from the customer's perspective, which means that, ideally, the users should have had a say before assigning a value to this criterion. That is, the market should have been assessed for a product to receive a high score.

High scores are assigned to products that are superior in the unique, differentiated category.

- *Attractive Market (Weight = 4):*

  An attractive market is one in which there is little or no competition and there are opportunities to sell high volumes and to earn high profits.

  The health care and medical markets are attractive to *Bargery Fabrics* because they already have a significant presence and expertise in these areas. These markets have high potential for growth and customers demand innovative products. In these markets, *Bargery Fabrics* can avoid highly competitive, low-cost, commodity products.

  Products in the health care market are technically challenging and subject to significant safety regulations. Thus, with a high barrier to entry into the market, there are opportunities for *Blue Ocean* products.

  High scores are assigned to products for which *Bargery Fabrics* perceives that there is an attractive market.

- *Capacity and Technical Feasibility (Weight = 3):*

  To give a high score to this criterion, the technical development of the product must seem promising, e.g., *Bargery Fabrics* has the technical capability to develop the product and the technical risk is low.[3]

  Additional positive aspects of this criterion are:

    - Time to Market: Scores are higher when the product can be introduced to the market quickly.[4]

    - The product makes good use of *Bargery Fabrics'* technical capabilities.

    - Low technical risk.

[3] Notice that this is an example of precisely defining the detailed aspects of a criterion, e.g., technical risk is assessed here, not financial risk.

[4] *Bargery Fabrics* needs some products with *early delivery* to generate income. Without this clarification, there might be confusion about in which criterion *early delivery* should be scored.

23

High scores are assigned to products for which *Bargery Fabrics* believes that they have good technical capabilities in this area.

- *Financial Attractiveness (Weight = 2 [5]):*

  Products that have a high financial attractiveness are those that with potential for high sales volumes, high Return on Investment (ROI), and high profitability. This criterion includes:

  - Financial return is high: high sales and strong margins.
  - Financial risk is low.
  - Production and support costs are low.

  High scores are assigned to products with a high potential for ROI.

- *Strategic Fit (Weight = 3):*

  This selection criterion measures the degree to which the product has synergies with other products, existing technical and marketing capabilities, and *Bargery Fabrics'* strategy. This includes, technical proficiency, staff, markets, and technology platforms. *Bargery Fabrics* can maximize its investment when products share technology platforms and markets.

  High scores are assigned to products with a good strategic fit and positive technical and marketing synergies.

5.1.2   Guidance on Assignment #1

Developing the selection criteria is an important step because it lays the foundation for what is to follow. Without a reasonable set of criteria the scoring matrix, and the resulting strategy, will not be effective. The selection criteria must be soundly based on the Critical Selection Factors (CSFs).

Therefore, while this is a relatively easy exercise, this assignment should not be rushed. The teams need time to acclimatize themselves to the topic, to become familiar with each other, and to establish group dynamics.

It is important to distinguish between the selection criteria (the assignment) and the Critical Success Factors (CSFs). The research has established the important attributes necessary for a successful commercial product—the CSFs. Therefore, the CSFs establish the important general issues that guide product selection.

The selection criteria are based on the CSFs, but are specific to *Bargery Fabrics*. Therefore, the selection criteria reflect *Bargery Fabrics'* specific goals, objectives and strategy.

[5]Notice the relatively low weight for this criterion, which reflects the research that shows the reduced importance of finance as a critical success factor.

24

Since a *unique, differentiated product* is such an important CSF, it becomes the most highly weighted selection criterion. At the other end of the scale, the *Financial Attractiveness* CSF is less important and carries a lower weight. The *attractive market* CSF is also important, but the criterion is made specific to *Bargery Fabrics* as the health care market. Products receive high scores only if they are in the health care market and attractive.

Early on, students should be encouraged to list all of the factors they think are important to *Bargery Fabrics.* Students should be encouraged to list product attributes and their descriptions and not just to list the criteria titles. They should document their discussion of the topics in each criterion so that when they come to score the products, and an issue arises, they will remember their rationale. Finally, they should group the topics to end up with 5-6 criteria.

For example, suppose a team wants to include a *Time to Market* criterion, which they decide is an important issue because *Bargery Fabrics* needs some early income. In which criterion should they score *Time to Market*? Adding a separate criterion may make their list too long. Therefore, defining *Time to Market* as part of the *Capacity and Technical Feasibility* criterion means that, during the scoring process, a shorter delivery time will enhance the *Capacity and Technical Feasibility* score.

The topic of *risk* often causes debate. Because *Bargery Fabrics* has a maturing product line, some students might want to add "risk" as a *positive* scoring criterion. The idea is that products that are riskier (and perhaps, therefore, more innovative) should get a higher score. However, a careful assessment of the word "risk" in this context might suggest that it is being confused with "innovation," and that higher scores should be assigned to more innovative products.

On the other hand, some students on the same team might see *risk* in its more traditional meaning, i.e., as a negative in that risky products may not meet their technical goals and should receive a lower score.

The way out of this dilemma is for the team to document carefully the details of the discussion about what goes into each criterion. For example, financial risk should be assessed as part of the *Financial Attractiveness* criterion, while technical risk should be assessed as part of the *Capacity and Technical Feasibility* criterion.

Completing the *selection matrix* is made easier when the team carefully defines how each criterion is scored. For example, one team created a criterion called *Competitive Advantage*, which they defined in Table 5.4.

Another team developed the set of criteria shown in Table 5.5, which links each selection criterion to a corresponding *Bargery Fabrics* strategic goal.[6]

[6]In Table 5.5 the weights have decimal values, which is not recommended because fractional weights require a detailed calibration using historical data. Predicting the future is generally not accurate enough to warrant such precision.

25

Table 5.4: Definition of the *Competitive Advantage* Criterion.

Score	0	4	7	10
Criterion				
Unique Customer Benefits	None	Limited	Some new benefits	Major new benefits
Value for money	Poor	Marginal	Good value	Great value
Customer View	Negative	Neutral	Positive	Great

Table 5.5: Scoring criteria explicitly linked to *Bargery Fabrics'* strategy.

Scoring Criteria	Weight
Innovative BF must open up new products and markets, their existing products are under threat.	5.0
Core Capabilities Matches BF's objectives and strategic plan, clear focus, technology base.	4.5
ROI As a medium sized company, BF investment must be cost effective.	2.5
Time to Market Increasingly important as BF products mature, and early income is necessary.	2.0

5.1.3   Questions for Assignment #1

Each team should present their rationale for choosing their selection criteria to the other teams. Asking the following questions helps to clarify that the students have understood the important concepts:

The relative importance of the CSFs:

- Are your selection criteria (roughly in order of importance): a unique differentiated product, an attractive market, clear product definition, financial attractiveness?

- Do your selection criteria reflect the priorities for the CSFs established in the research?

- Do your weights correctly reflect the relative importance of the CSFs?

- Is a *unique, differentiated product* one of your most important selection criteria?

- Is *Return on Investment (ROI)* a relatively low priority selection criterion?

Bargery Fabrics' strategy and goals should be reflected in the selection criteria:

- Do your selection criteria reflect the company's desire to focus on the hygiene and health care markets?

- Is the desire for new and innovative products reflected in your weights?

- Do your weights reflect the goal of avoiding commodity products and price sensitive markets?

5.2 Assignment #2

Complete the Portfolio Selection Matrix.

For all products, assign a score to each selection criterion and calculate its total score.

5.2.1 Solution to Assignment #2

The students should score all of the products for the criteria defined in Assignment #1 using score from 0–10.[7] Students should ensure that all scoring is done in the *same* direction and that higher scores favor selection.

This one of the longer assignments and handing out a blank Excel spreadsheet with the scoring formulas in place will expedite this assignment.

Table 5.6 presents a reasonable solution. Students will be expected to defend their selection matrix and an easy way to present the essential information is to use numbered notes in the table to illustrate important, or significant, team decisions. For example, the (*1) in the *ROI* column for *First Aid Dressings* documents the team's decision to give a low score to *ROI* because it is a commodity product, the market is highly competitive, and low margins are predicted.

[7]Scores out of 10 are less likely to produce bunching of results than 0–5.

27

Table 5.6: Assignment # 2: Sample Selection Matrix.

Selection Criteria	Unique Product	Attractive Market	Capacity, Technical Feasibility	Return on Invest.	Strategic Fit	Total Score
Weight	5	4	3	2	3	
Product						
1) First Aid Dressings	5	3	8	3 (*1)	1 (*2)	70
2) Orthopedic Padding	7 0	5	2	1	4	75
3) Wound Dressings	8	9 (*3)	7	8	8	137
4) Gowns & Drapes	6	1	9	4 (*4)	4	81
5) Face Masks	0	1	7	3	0	31
6) Replaceable Insoles	1	0	6	5	0	33
7) Sports & Leisurewear	2	1 (*5)	2	2	0	24
8) Protective Garments	8	6	6	5	9	119
9) Hospital Bedding	6	6	7	7	6	107
9) Domestic Bedding	2	1	7	4	2	49
11) Smart Materials	7	7 (*6)	5	3	7	105
12) Silver monitoring	0 (*7)	0	10	0	1	60

An example of the scoring calculation is shown below. In each pair, the first number is the weight and the second is the product score.

First Aid Dressings: 5x5 + 4x3 + 3x8 + 2x3 + 3x1 = 70
Orthopedic padding: 5x7 + 4x5 + 3x2 + 2x1 + 3x4 = 75

Typical notes are as follows:

(*1) The low score for *ROI* is because *First Aid Dressings* is a commodity product, the market is highly competitive, and low margins are predicted.

(*2) The low score for *First Aid Dressings* in the *Strategic Fit* criterion is because it is the only product using the bio-actives platform. It has little technical synergy with other products.

(*3) These high scores for *Wound Dressings* all reflect the fact that the case makes clear that *Bargery Fabrics* considers this product as critical to its future.

(*4) The low scores for *Gowns & Drapes* reflect the fact that this product uses a licensed technology, which means that *Bargery Fabrics* does not control the technology and, because of license fees, that the margins are potentially lower. On the other hand, this product is ready to enter the market.

(*5) The low scores for *Sports & Leisurewear* reflect a commodity product in a price-competitive market.

(*6) The scores for *Smart Materials* reflect the fact that the product is technically very innovative and aligns well with *Bargery Fabrics'* long-term strategy. However, the product is some years away and, therefore, technical performance and marketing data are speculative and uncertain.

(*7) The zeroes for *Silver Monitoring* reflect the fact that it is not a commercial product and will generate no sales or income. It is a *compliance* product.

5.2.2 Guidance on Assignment #2

This assignment will take a considerable amount of time and the instructor must keep the teams moving along. After a few minutes in which the students learn how to assign scores, it is useful to ask them if the process might be accomplished more efficiently.

One approach is for the teams to assign one or two team members as "experts" on a particular selection criterion (e.g., market attractiveness) and they then score all the products in that criterion. This speeds up the process by allowing the scores to be developed in parallel and also helps to ensure consistency in the scoring.

Students should be encouraged to be tough graders. That is, they should avoid the tendency to give many 5s and 6s. Only a few, really exceptional, products should get a 9 or 10. Students should not be afraid to give 2s and 3s to poor products. This separates the total scores and makes the following steps much easier.

Students should realize that products with total scores that are close should be treated equally. In the Table 5.6, #10 *Hospital Bedding*, with a score of 107, should be considered to be essentially equivalent to #11 *Smart Materials*, with a score of 105.

Students should be also made aware that changing one score in a single category can have a marked effect on the scores and rankings. For example, changing the score of the *Smart Materials* product in the *unique* criterion from a 7 to a 9 increases its total score to 115. This vaults *Smart Materials* over *Hospital Bedding*, which may be significant in the allocation of funds.

Therefore, all individual scores for products with similar total scores should be re-evaluated for consistency. This is referred to as a sensitivity analysis.

The total scores are sensitive to the values of the weights. Students should be encouraged to investigate small changes to the value of one or two of the weights and to determine if that has a significant impact on the product order. If so, is the new order more appropriate?

5.2.3 Questions for Assignment #2

Each team should present their *selection matrix* along with their rationale for selecting the scores. Questions that help to clarify the important conceptual concepts include:

- Do your scores show a significant variation? Are there 2s and 9s?

- How do you justify your high scores?

- How do you justify your low scores?

- Which products have essentially the same score?

- How do your rankings vary if you change a few, critical scores?

5.3 Assignment # 3

Allocate the budget to the top products.

Sort the selection matrix so that the products with the highest scores are at the top. Allocate funds until the product development budget of $600,000 is consumed.

5.3.1 Solution to Assignment #3

Product development costs are given in Table 3.2. Students should calculate the costs required for the *first year* only. Products are not guaranteed to be funded in future years and, so, only next year's funding is considered.

The total budget assigned to new products is $600,000. The students should iden-
tify the cut-off point where projects can no longer be funded.

A possible solution is shown in Table 5.7.

Table 5.7: Assignment # 3: Solution for the Budget Assignment.

Criteria	Score high to low	Next Year's Request	Cumulative Allocation
Product			
Wound Dressings	137	170	170
Protective Garments	119	120	290
Hospital Bedding	107	120	410
Smart Materials	105	90	500
Gowns & Drapes	81	50	550
Orthopedic Padding	75	100	650
		Total Budget	$600K
First Aid Dressings	70		
Silver Monitoring	60		
Domestic Bedding	49		
Replaceable Insoles	33		
Face Masks	31		
Sports & Leisurewear	24		

5.3.2 Guidance on Assignment #3

This is a relatively straightforward assignment. However, it is important to emphasize that only project costs for the first year are included in the table. This
is because projects are typically funded on a year-by-year basis and no project is
guaranteed to be funded next year. If a project performs poorly, it may be canceled.

While the portfolio is dynamic, the total budget is fixed by senior management and is not negotiable. This means that the evolution of the portfolio only results in the re-distribution of funds between products without changing the total. This approach reflects the standard PPM approach in which there is a yearly product evaluation cycle. A more dynamic, continuous evaluation of products takes place at Panaz, which is described in Chapter 6.

Strategic issues can affect which products will be funded. To illustrate this, we temporarily ignore the above list and imagine that the total scores looked like Table 5.8.

Table 5.8: Alternative budget table detail

Product	Score	Budget	Cumulative
⋮	⋮	⋮	⋮
#2 Hospital Bedding	88	$120K	$500K
#5 Face Masks	75	$100K	$600K
		Budget Reached	$600K
#10 Domestic Bedding	73	$120K	

We observe that *Hospital Bedding* is well above the funding line and selected for development. Its high scores reflect the fact that it is an excellent match to the company's proposed strategy, i.e., moving to the health care market.

In this instance, a strict application of the rule that one should select the products with the highest scores would mean that *Face Masks* would also be funded, but *Domestic Bedding* would not. However, *Face Masks* and *Domestic Bedding* have total scores that are essentially equivalent and a small change to the individual scores for either product might change the order.[8]

Therefore, it is legitimate to ask if there are reasons, besides their scores, for deciding whether *Face Masks* or *Domestic Bedding* should be funded.

We note that *Domestic Bedding* and *Hospital Bedding* are similar technical products, but compete in different markets. Therefore, there is significant synergy between them. In which case, one might re-examine the scores and the synergy might increase the scores for *Domestic Bedding*, moving it above *Face Masks*. One might also argue that *Face Masks* does not fit with the goals of the company as it is a commodity product in a highly competitive market.

[8]One should not take the accuracy of the process too literally.

Another approach might be to simply combine the bedding products and not fund *Face Masks*. The justification would be that *Hospital Bedding* is an excellent match to the company's strategy and *Domestic Bedding* could share the development platform. While *Domestic Bedding* is in a competitive market, it might be valuable if considered as a low cost extension to *Hospital Bedding*.

Recognizing the synergy between the hospital and domestic bedding products, the committee might just direct the product managers to come up with a joint effort.

It often comes as a surprise to students, but less so to company learners, that neither the projects nor the budgets are sacred. That is, the portfolio selection team can, and often does, adjust products and budgets to meet strategic goals.[9]

In practice, it is not unusual for products with relatively high budget requests to suffer cuts. Perhaps cutting all projects by 15% can generate enough funds for an extra, attractive project. Or, a single, very expensive project towards the bottom of the selected list might be eliminated to make room for several attractive, smaller candidates.

For example, the *Domestic Bedding* and *Hospital Bedding* projects are both high cost, but are technically very similar. Therefore, cutting out the *Domestic Bedding* and combining the projects might be a viable option.[10]

It should be continually reinforced that portfolio management is not an exact science. One is attempting to predict the future, which is difficult at best. In practice, the publication of the final matrix will have a significant impact throughout the company and it will be carefully scrutinized. The selection committee needs to ensure that everyone will understand the rationale for which products were selected.[11]

As well as selecting the funded products for next year, it is equally important to recognize that the *selection matrix* communicates the company's future goals and objectives. Managers whose products were not selected can improve their products for next year's selection cycle. Overall, therefore, the company's products improve, and according to the explicitly defined objectives.

Another way to avoid obvious mistakes is to "kill the dogs." Many companies take on too many products and, despite getting poor results, still fail to stop investing in them. The *selection matrix* makes obvious which products are the worst performers.

There is often considerable debate about the *Smart Materials* product, which is a long-term research project, but is often regarded as innovative and attractive. However, since the product's delivery is so far in the future, the marketing data is highly suspect.[12]

Therefore, one approach is to cut the budget for this product[13] and to refine the

[9]Note: The selection committee is not passive, they actively manage the products and strategy. For another excellent example of committee activeness, see section 6.3, *The Nano Project*.

[10]These strategic budget adjustments are previews of the types of actions that are to come when we develop the roadmap, Assignment #5.

[11]Despite this, one should expect a lot of hurt feelings around the coffee pot.

[12]Also, truly innovative products are often poorly understood.

[13]Academic research budgets are often cut.

project as follows. First, ask the university to develop a prototype and for the researchers to assess the technical performance characteristics and risks. Second, given the potential technical performance, conduct a marketing study to determine the product's market potential. These deliverables should be completed in time for the next product evaluation cycle.

Note that the selection committee is proactive. They re-define product content (the technical goals), specify future deliveries (marketing studies), and propose the schedule (products to be available for the next decision cycle).[14]

Finally, one has to recognize that the *Silver Monitoring* project is a compliance project and must be funded.[15]

At this point, an adjusted set of products to be funded should be proposed along with the supporting strategy.[16]

5.3.3   Questions for Assignment #3

Questions that help to clarify the important conceptual concepts include:

- The Budget

  - Did you modify any of the proposed product budgets?
  - Did you move any products into or out of the funded list? Why?
  - Did you fund *Silver Monitoring*, which must be funded because it is a compliance project?
  - Did you adjust the requested funds for *Smart Materials*?

- The Strategy[17]

  - Is your product list consistent with the company's strategy?
  - Are *Bargery Fabrics'* most critical products at the top of your list?

5.4   Assignment #4

Recommend a Product Strategy for Bargery Fabrics.

[14]In a dynamic portfolio, these activities are continuous, rather than yearly.

[15]Even though it generates no income.

[16]At this stage, the committee's activities are somewhat *ad hoc.* They will become formal when we cover *Dynamic Portfolio Management.*

[17]This will be further developed in Assignment #4.

34

5.4.1 Solution to Assignment #4

The proposed list of projects should be analyzed, along with the scores, to determine if the list agrees with the articulated *Bargery Fabrics* strategy. An important consideration is that budgets are estimates and students should feel free to make strategically justified changes to the funding requests.

The proposed products should all be health care related so that they support the new mission of the company, which is to focus on the markets where *Bargery Fabrics* can make unique, high value-added products.

Table 5.9: Assignment 4: Adjusted Product Strategy.

Criteria	Score high to low	Next Year's Request	Note	Cumulative Allocation
Proposed Products				
Silver Monitoring	60	50	(*1)	50
Wound Dressings	137	160	(*2)	210
Protective Garments	119	120		330
Hospital Bedding	107	120		450
Smart Materials	105	50	(*3)	500
Gowns & Drapes	81	0	(*4)	500
Orthopedic Padding	75	100		600
Domestic Bedding	49	0	(*6)	

Table 5.9 contains some suggested adjustments to the *selection matrix*, which are documented in the following notes.

(*1) *Silver Monitoring:*

This is a "compliance project," which means that it must be completed to comply with the new government regulations. Therefore, despite its score, it was moved to the top of the list.

(*2) *Wound Dressings:*

35

It was made clear that this is an important product in the *Bargery Fabrics* strategy. It should appear towards the top of the list.

(*3) *Smart Materials:*

This is a university research project and is speculative. Therefore, the budget was cut to $50K and the project redefined. The university will be charged with developing a prototype product to establish technical feasibility and conducting a marketing study.

The outcomes are to be a demonstration product with an assessment of its likelihood of technical success, a projected time-frame, and a preliminary market assessment. If the prototype is encouraging, next year's budget can be increased.

(*4) *Gowns & Drapes:*

After re-examining the scores, the team observed that the reason this project scored so high was almost entirely due to the score of "9" assigned to *Technical Feasibility*, which is due to it being a licensed product. All other scores were quite mediocre. If the technical feasibility score were changed, the product would not be funded.

The technical risk for this project is, indeed, low because it is a licensed product that is ready for release. Therefore, the score of "9" is appropriate. However, because of license fees, the product has low profit margins and *Bargery Fabrics* currently has no presence in the market. Finally, as a licensed product, *Bargery Fabrics* has little control over the technology platform.

Therefore, a re-evaluation of this product suggests that, overall, it was not very attractive and should not be funded. Funds were freed up for other products.

(*5) *Orthopedic Padding:*

Because of the elimination of the *Gowns & Drapes* product, the *Orthopedic Padding* project can now be funded. From a strategic perspective, this is a reasonable approach because the *Orthopedic Padding* product is much more in line with the company's goals and objectives.

With the above adjustments, the total budget of the selected projects was $610K, which was $10K over the allocation. Therefore, the project with the largest budget (*Wound Dressings*) was cut by $10K, from $170K to $160K.

(*6) *Domestic Bedding:*

> This product was not funded. However, its score was not that far from the funding line and it has significant synergy with the *Hospital Bedding* product, which was funded. Since they are very similar products, but with different markets, a joint project might be proposed.
>
> This could be accomplished as follows:
>
> - The two project managers could be ordered to come up with a joint project.
> - The *Hospital Bedding* product could go ahead and the *Domestic Bedding* product could continue with a low-cost marketing study. The goal would be to see if the *Hospital Bedding* technology could be quickly adapted, at low cost, to the domestic market.

Almost all of the proposed products are consistent with *Bargery Fabrics* strategy of moving towards the health care market. The exception is *Protective Garments*, but this is a unique product with the potential to create an entirely new market.[18] It also has significant technical synergy with other products and technology platforms.

5.4.2 Guidance on Assignment #4

This assignment requires the students to analyze the portfolio and to present their results. The goal is not simply to list the products to be funded, but to present a coherent strategy. The strategy sessions build vocabulary and enhance student understanding of the theoretical concepts.

Since *Bargery Fabrics'* product lines are maturing, the company needs to invest in innovative products. However, they cannot afford to invest only in products with a long term payoff because the decline in income from maturing products must be offset by income from a few new products. Therefore, part of the strategy should be to fund some products that can be brought to market quickly.

There are two additional themes the students need to be aware of in their final strategy: the markets and the technology platforms. Marketing is more efficient when multiple products share the same market space. It is also more cost effective when multiple products share the same underlying technology platform. These issues can be assessed after the products have been scored.

Bargery Fabrics believes that *Wound Dressings* is their most important product. Student scores should reflect this data and this product should have risen towards the top of the list.

[18]A Blue Ocean Strategy.

The *Gowns and Drapes* product often turns out to be one of the borderline selections and one on which there is debate and disagreement. The issues are that, while potential sales are high, *Bargery Fabrics* has little control over the technology platform because it is a licensed technology. They have no presence in the market and, because they have to pay license fees, it has low profit margins. On the other hand, the *Gowns and Drapes* product has the potential for quick deployment and might be prioritized if the portfolio needs a product with short-term return.

A careful analysis of the justification for the *Gowns and Drapes* product is likely to produce an interesting discussion.

Several products, such as *Face Masks*, are in highly competitive, low-cost markets, which are unattractive to *Bargery Fabrics*. These products should receive low scores in the *ROI* and *Uniqueness* categories. As a result, they should appear towards the bottom of the list.[19]

Moving to Dynamic Portfolio Management

The students' strategic analysis should demonstrate that their portfolio supports the *Bargery Fabrics* strategy as articulated in the case. While their assessment of the portfolio is undoubtedly useful, the process might seem rather *ad hoc* in that they have been given no specific guidance about how to perform the strategic analysis. Also, their portfolio is considered to be static as it will not change until next year's evaluation cycle is completed.

This lack of a strategic assessment tools and the static view of the products is a major criticism of classic portfolio management. In Assignment #5, we will introduce *Dynamic Portfolio Management*, which addresses these issues by providing methods for the dynamic evaluation of product content and for the strategic assessment of the portfolio.[20]

5.4.3 Questions for Assignment #4

Each team analyses the product list for consistency with the *Bargery Fabrics* strategy. Questions that help to clarify the important conceptual concepts, include:

- Strategy

    - Are your products clearly in the health care market?

    - Do some of your products produce short term income?

    - *Bargery Fabrics* believes that wound dressings are their most important product. Is this product near the top of your list?

[19]These tend to be the commodity products.

[20]The Panaz case (Chapter 6, section 6.1) shows how *Dynamic Portfolio Management* can support the continuous evaluation of products in a real company.

- Technology and Marketing Synergies

  - Do any of your products use only one technology platform?
  - Do any of your products use multiple technology platforms?
  - Can any of your products combine marketing efforts?

- Commodity Products

  - Are any of your products commodities in competitive markets?
  - Are commodity products at the bottom of your list?

5.5 Assignment #5

Assess the portfolio and develop a roadmap.

Present the portfolio to upper management along with the rationale.

5.5.1 Solution to Assignment #5

The Highlights of Dynamic Portfolio Management

We begin by presenting the highlights of *Dynamic Portfolio Management.* The dynamism of a portfolio is divided into two categories: internal and external.[21]

Therefore, the solution is divided into two parts:

1. Assess the internal dynamics of the portfolio and produce a preliminary roadmap.

2. Assess the dynamics of the company's external environment and produce the final roadmap.

The dynamism in the portfolio's internal, operational aspects leads to adapting the technical content and internal reconfiguration of the products, e.g., responding to evolving customer requirements, canceling projects, re-prioritizing funds, etc.

Internal to the portfolio, the activities are:

- *Sensing:* Mechanisms to identify and interpret changes within the portfolio.

- *Seizing:* Mechanisms for deciding on changes within portfolio (once the need has been sensed).

[21]A summary of the key ideas in *Dynamic Portfolio Management* research is presented in Chapter 8, Research.

39

- *Reconfiguring:* The actual reconfiguration of the portfolio, which is accomplished by adding (or removing) resources (people, funds); dividing products into multiple, smaller deliveries; adding and deleting content; and re-prioritizing products.[22]

The dynamism in the portfolio's external business environment leads to transforming of the company processes, e.g., re-defining corporate strategies, the introduction of new processes, and adapting to the evolution of markets.

External to the portfolio, the activities are:

- *Sensing:* Mechanisms to identify and interpret changes that affect the business.

- *Seizing:* Mechanisms for deciding on changes to the business (once the need has been sensed).

- *Transforming:* The actual reconfiguration of the business. Transforming is accomplished by updating strategy, changing processes, and re-prioritizing markets.

In both cases, the result is an evolution of the product roadmap, which displays the schedule of key product content deliveries over time. The roadmap shows the dependencies between products and their underlying technology platforms. For example, it might show where early successes from one product could be transferable to another. The roadmap also highlights the importance of marketing activities as a means of focusing technical development.

Finally, indicating product launches on the roadmap identifies when the income begins to flow in from each project, thus linking the product strategy to the financial picture.

These general characteristics of DPM are made specific to *Bargery Fabrics* in the following sections.

Assessing the Internal Dynamics of the Portfolio

The students should begin the assessment of the internal dynamics of their portfolio by producing a preliminary roadmap from their selected products and the associated delivery schedules given in section 3.2.

For each product, students should show the following milestones: the completion of product development, the completion of user trials, and the product launch. Quarterly time units are sufficient.

[22]We saw examples of these activities in Assignment #4.

Fig. 5.1 gives an example of a preliminary roadmap, which presents the schedule data in graphical form. Many synergies and interactions between the products should become clear from the roadmap. The symbols in Fig. 5.1 are defined in Fig. 5.2

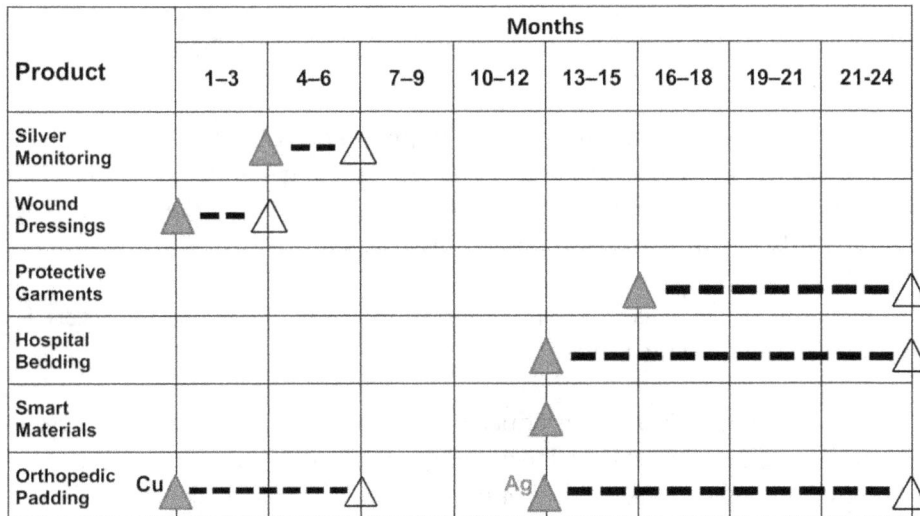

Product	Months							
	1–3	4–6	7–9	10–12	13–15	16–18	19–21	21-24
Silver Monitoring		▲--△						
Wound Dressings	▲--△							
Protective Garments						▲------------△		
Hospital Bedding					▲------------------△			
Smart Materials					▲			
Orthopedic Padding	Cu ▲------△				Ag ▲------------------△			

Figure 5.1: Preliminary Roadmap.

Symbol	Meaning
▲	Completion of Product Development
- - -	User Trials
△	Product Launch
Cu	Copper Technology Platform
Ag	Silver Technology Platform

Figure 5.2: Symbols used in the preliminary roadmap.

Next, the students should present their roadmap, along with its supporting rationale, and demonstrate how their selected products meet the strategic goals of *Bargery Fabrics*.

41

We begin with *Sensing*, i.e., identifying and interpreting potential changes within the portfolio.

- The *Wound Dressings* product has an early launch and is *Bargery Fabrics'* first product to market that uses the metalized silver fibers technology platform. This technology should be monitored closely as there may be applications to other products.

  This is a significant and positive development because it is one of the highest priority products for *Bargery Fabrics*. It will generate early sales, thus eliminating the necessity of introducing a lower scoring (i.e., less strategically valuable) product to generate early sales.

- It should also be clear that the important product, *Protective Garments*, is a long way off into the future.

- The *Orthopedic Padding* product has two separate technology deliveries, one using the copper-based technology (Cu) and the other using the silver-based technology (Ag). The copper platform is almost ready for use and, so, it is recommended that the product be separated into two distinct deliveries.[23]

- The metalized fiber technology platforms are indicated by *Ag* and *Cu* and the arrows denote possible synergy between the products.

  For example, the *Wound Dressings* product uses *Ag* and will be completed by month 3. It is possible, therefore, that the *Hospital Bedding* product can take advantage of this to advance its launch date. This is indicated by an arrow in Fig. 5.3.

As a result of the above sensing analysis, the following updates are proposed for the portfolio. (*Seizing*)

- Closely monitor *Wound Dressings*. It is a critical product and emerged as one of the top products in the selection matrix.

- The above sensing analysis suggests that it might be possible to divide the entire portfolio into deliveries that are associated with their technology platforms.

[23]Also requiring two market studies.

- The silver technology platform is ready to be deployed and may advance the delivery of other products, particularly *Protective Garments* and *Hospital Bedding.* Therefore, it is proposed to establish cooperation between the projects that use the sliver technology (see arrows in Fig. 5.3).

- Accelerate the *Orthopedic Padding* product, as it is nearly ready to go into user trials:

    - Establish cooperation with the *Protective Garments* product (see arrow in Fig. 5.3).

- The *Protective Garments* product has a very long time line and will not produce income for at least another two years. Therefore, the product might be divided into several sub-deliveries, each with its own technology platform and potential market:

    - Determine if intermediate deliverables might be viable products. For example, add a silver anti-microbial middle layer to existing garments to produce a unique and valuable product.

    - Establish cooperation with other projects (see arrows).

    - Explore the possibility of earlier deliveries of partial products using the available technologies.

    - Conduct a market assessment in preparation for next year's product evaluations. This should be delivered in month 9 so that the results are available for next year's evaluations.

After a review of the above *Seizing* issues, it was decided to implement the following actions: (*Reconfiguring*)

- Accelerate the *Orthopedic Padding* product using the copper technology.

- Since wound dressings with the silver technology is nearly ready to launch, conduct marketing studies on the possibility of intermediate deliveries of silver-based products for hospital bedding, protective garments, and orthopedic padding products.

- For the *Smart Materials* product, propose that the market study and the technical feasibility assessment be completed by month nine, so that they are available for next year's portfolio product evaluations.

- Study whether it is possible to accelerate the *Hospital Bedding* product using the silver technology from the wound dressings product, which is ready to go into user trials:

- Establish cooperation between the projects using the silver technology and explore the possibility of earlier delivery of partial products using the available silver technology.

- The micro-encapsulation technology platform is used in several products and is indicated on the final roadmap by μ. We observe that most of the products that could use the micro-encapsulation technology are not immediately available—they are out at least 12 months.

  Therefore, the funding for this technology could be reduced to a monitoring role. Before next years portfolio evaluation, the company might request a technology and market study that evaluates the potential impact of micro-encapsulation on the products that were funded this year.[24]

All of these issues can be indicated on the final roadmap, which is shown in Fig. 5.3. The symbols in Fig. 5.3 are defined in Fig. 5.4

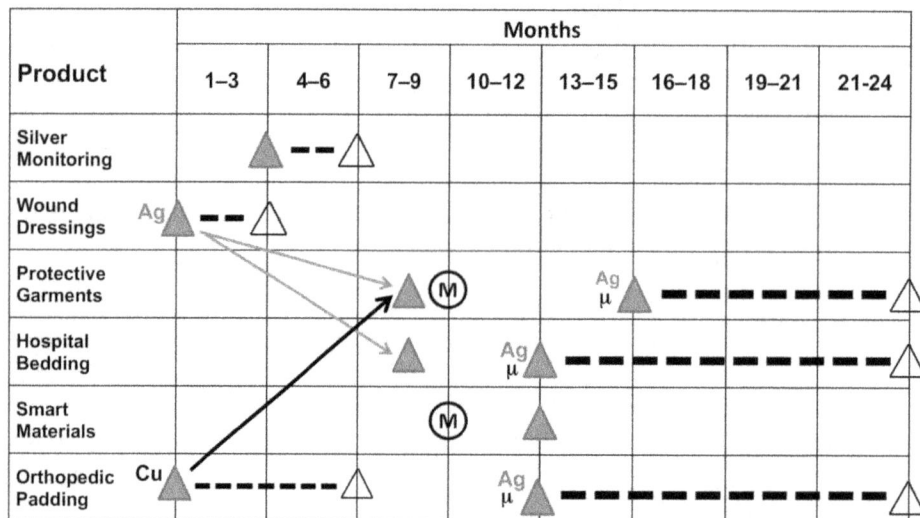

Figure 5.3: Final Roadmap.

[24]This is an example of how the roadmap helps to make visible the strategic interactions between technologies and markets.

Symbol	Meaning
▲	Completion of Product Development
━ ━ ━	User Trials
△	Product Launch
Ⓜ	Marketing Study
Cu	Copper Technology Platform
Ag	Silver Technology Platform
μ	Micro-encapsulation Platform
⟶	Copper Technology Transfer
⟶	Silver Technology Transfer

Figure 5.4: Symbols used in the final roadmap.

Assessing the External Dynamics of the Portfolio

We begin by identifying and interpreting potential changes external to the portfolio. The *Silver Monitoring* project is an excellent example of an external factor with a direct impact on the portfolio. The project arises from the introduction of new regulations and must be funded, despite providing no income.

The roadmap improves visibility into management processes external to the portfolio. For example, dividing products into multiple deliveries requires close coordination between the technical and marketing departments of multiple products. This is an example of how the introduction of a portfolio management system can affect the structure of the company and how the departments interact.[25]

Corporate research budgets frequently change in response to the company's financial performance, market forces, and strategic initiatives, all of which may also affect the portfolio.

The dynamic assessment of the external impacts on *Bargery Fabrics* begins by studying changes external to the portfolio. (*Sensing*)

- Government regulations in this area are increasing and more data collection and reporting is likely.

- The company is investing in multiple technology platforms. Are they all appropriate?

As a result of the above sensing analysis, the following updates are proposed for the portfolio. (*Seizing*)

[25]See the Panaz case for an example of this, section 6.2.

45

- Explain to the Information Technology (IT) department that increasing regulation is likely and they should design flexibility into the silver monitoring project. They should consider making a more general-purpose product that can accommodate multiple types of reports applicable to different compounds.

- It would be useful to assess the long-term potential of the various technology platforms in the health care market.

After a review of the above *Seizing* issues, it was decided to implement the following actions. (*Transforming*)

- The Information Technology (IT) department will design a general-purpose software application that can produce the required reports for many types of regulated compounds.

- Improve the management processes at *Bargery Fabrics*, particularly the interactions between the technical and marketing departments. This might include documenting the processes recently completed and setting up a portfolio management committee.

- Conduct a market study for the micro-encapsulation technology platform to determine where best to target funds.

These issues should be indicated on the final roadmap.

5.5.2 Guidance on Assignment #5

The above sections are an excellent example of DPM in action.

The roadmap is a compilation of the schedules for the selected products (the top scorers in the selection matrix). The overall goal of the final roadmap is to ensure that the resulting portfolio satisfies the company's strategic goals.

The students should *analyze* the final roadmap and this is where the dynamic aspects of the process come into play. For example, products may be broken up into smaller components and the interactions with marketing studies become relevant. Such actions can accelerate deliveries, produce earlier revenue, provide more visibility into synergy between products, generate more relevant marketing data, and enhance cooperation between customers and products.

Another characteristic of DPM that emerges is the cooperation and interaction between products. By acknowledging the common technology platforms, it is recognized that the silver technology is almost ready in the *Wound Dressings* product and the results might be transferable to other products.

The same applies to the copper technology in the *Orthopedic Padding* product, which might be transferable to *Protective Garments*.

The importance of marketing studies emerged as a means of focusing the technical development. Several products combine multiple technologies and, by adding strategic marketing studies, *Bargery Fabrics* might be able to decide whether there are viable products that could be delivered earlier and produce revenue.

Products that have deliveries well into the future may be broken up into multiple deliveries, the viability of which can be enhanced by a market study. For example, the *Protective Garments* product might be restructured before next year's request for funds, which will require a marketing study to be completed by month nine.

DPM promotes an active and cooperative management approach.

- Cooperation between product managers is required, not just encouraged, by the synergies between the products, their technology platforms, and marketing.

- The portfolio committee actively adapts the products and deliveries. For example, the *Smart Materials* product was re-defined as an exploratory, prototype development and a marketing study was added.

- Formally presenting the roadmap to upper management gives visibility into the evolving strategy. By approving the new portfolio, upper management explicitly communicates the strategy throughout the company.

The Roadmap

The creation of the roadmap, and its review by upper management, completes the assessment of the strategy.

The roadmap shows the schedule of deliverables for the products over time, which immediately illustrates a number of important issues. For example, one can immediately answer the question: Does the proposed portfolio generate early income, which is a strategic priority for the company.

The roadmap facilitates the dividing of products into smaller deliveries by making visible which products have long timescales. Creating smaller projects, with more

47

frequent deliveries, improves the project management process. The status of the product can be assessed more accurately through the technical, marketing, and strategic evaluation of intermediate deliverables.

The roadmap also makes clear when there is synergy between projects that use the same technology platforms. It is a small step, therefore, for the students to realize that they can take advantage of early deliveries of one product to advance another one.

It is not unusual for teams to mark up the roadmap using creative graphics to represent useful information, e.g., the relations between products, common platforms, and delivery of marketing information. We have tried to show some examples of these ideas in Fig. 5.3:

- the addition of the copper (Cu) and silver (Ag) platforms.

- arrows showing inter-dependencies between products

- different icons for product status milestones: start of development, delivery of prototype, launch into the market.

- milestones for the delivery of marketing information

Teams should be encouraged to dress up their roadmaps as they will become the primary communication tool for discussions about the portfolio and, by implication, the company strategy. In companies, the roadmap and will generally be made available throughout the company.

5.5.3 Questions for Assignment #5

Questions that help to clarify the important conceptual concepts, include:

- Is your portfolio balanced?

  To answer this question the students need to be able to show that their portfolio has the following characteristics:

  - A balance of new and innovative products vs. existing and revenue producing products. Existing lines produce revenue now, while future revenues will come from new, innovative products.

  - A balance of platforms. A platform that supports several products is more economical, but risks are mitigated by using several platforms.

48

- A balance of corporate strategies. Products should reflect multiple corporate goals and objectives.

- Have you broken up the projects with long delivery schedules into smaller products with multiple, earlier deliveries?

  - Can any of your products be broken up into independent, stand-alone products?

  - How do you ensure that your products are technically achievable and have value to your customers?

- What is the relation between your markets and your technology platforms?

  - Do you have multiple products that are sold in the same market space?

  - Do you have multiple products that use the same underlying technology?

  - Did you select the band aids product, which is the only one to use the Bio-Active Coatings technology?

- Is your roadmap consistent with the *Bargery Fabrics* strategy?

  - What is the contribution of your products to the company strategy?

  - Is your portfolio balanced?

  - Where is the customer feedback in your roadmap?

  - Do you have visibility into intermediate deliverables?

5.6   General Issues

In this section we cover some of the general issues that arise during student discussions about the dynamic portfolio.

5.6.1   An Open Process

One of the most valuable aspects of the portfolio management process is that it should be completely open, i.e., the process is visible to everyone in the company.

This encourages debate and helps to avoid conflict by explaining the rationale for which products were selected. The company roadmap communicates to managers what deliverables are required and when.

It is not unusual for managers of products that were not selected to read the reviews of their proposed product and to adapt their approach by rewriting their technical and marketing plans. The goal is to get their product onto the funded list in future rounds of the selection process. Thus, the visibility of the process encourages fair competition and the company, as a whole, benefits.

5.6.2 Everything in the Portfolio

It is important to stress that all products requiring investment funds should be included in the portfolio. For example, the *Silver Monitoring* project is not a new technology product, but a government mandated requirement. Since it will not produce any sales or profits, one might ask if it really belongs in the list of new technology products?

Even though it is not a new product, the *Silver Monitoring* project competes for the same funds and the same limited company resources (staff, laboratory time, and equipment). Therefore, the *Silver Monitoring* project should not be hidden, but tracked and managed like all the other projects.

Such projects are referred to as *compliance projects* and all such projects should be included in the portfolio so that the resources can be tracked and managed.

Adding compliance projects to the selection process also highlights their role and allows the delivery of content and the schedule to be managed and displayed in the roadmap. The fact that *Silver Monitoring* was likely to be the first of many such projects became clear when it was added to the roadmap. As a result of the analysis, the *Silver Monitoring* product was upgraded to become a more generally useful product.

For compliance projects, like all other projects, funds can be moved and deliveries adjusted to further the company's strategic goals. This would not be possible of the compliance projects were not visible in the selection process.

5.6.3 Market Data

Market data has to be considered as indicative only because it is a projection into the future, which is always highly uncertain. Also, projected large sales volumes are not necessarily sufficient, as the profit margin must be taken into account. For example, sportswear volumes are high, but the market is price sensitive (low margins) and very competitive.

5.6.4 Alternative Approaches

The students will derive different approaches based on their reading of the case, their selection criteria, and their product scores. Therefore, it is important to emphasize the *Bargery Fabrics* strategy as detailed in Chapter 1. As in all case analyses, student conclusions should be based firmly on the actual data.

Students should be encouraged to perform a sensitivity analysis in which scores and weights are slightly changed and the impact assessed. If the portfolio changes significantly, then they need to perform a more careful analysis. Some care must be taken when changing the weights, which have a significant impact on the total scores. If the sensitivity analysis does not change the results significantly, this helps to establish the validity of their answers and the results can be presented with confidence.

5.6.5 The Timescale for Portfolio Evaluation

Only project costs for the first year are included in the funding decision, see Table 5.7. By selecting a yearly review cycle, we followed a fairly traditional approach to PPM in which companies often perform a yearly review of their portfolio and fund projects on a regular schedule.[26]

It is essential to understand projects are not guaranteed long-term funding. Many projects will present a time-line that goes forward several years, but if it performs poorly, either technically or in the market, it may be canceled. Other, more suitable, products may replace it in the portfolio.

Longer-term projects face internal and external challenges. The internal challenge is that of effective project management, which includes delivering the promised technical content on time and within budget. While the desired content, budget, and schedule will all evolve, the development team must continuously convince the portfolio evaluation team that the product is unique, differentiated, and of value to customers.

The second challenge for long-term projects is that they must adapt to external forces, such as market evolution, improved products from competitors, and business climate changes. The evolution of the external environment can dramatically change the assessment of the uniqueness of the technical product and of its market attractiveness.

Therefore, all funded products compete in the next cycle where they will be evaluated based on both their project management (technical accomplishment of con-

[26]In companies, the new product evaluation is usually conducted on a yearly cycle that coincides with the budget cycle.

51

tent, cost, and schedule) and their ability to satisfy the evolved market and the updated corporate strategic goals.

Traditionally, portfolio evaluation was conducted on a yearly basis. However, recent research has shown that portfolios are dynamic and companies have begun to take a more flexible approach. Chapter 6, Implementation, describes a company that conducts a continuous review of products.

5.6.6   Evaluating the Middle Products

In many companies, the products that end up at the top and at the bottom of the selection matrix are quite predictable. In reality, everyone has a pretty good appreciation for which of their products are the winners and which are the dogs. Therefore, an intense debate often centers around the products in the middle of the selection matrix.

The debate about products in the middle of the selection matrix will often evoke emotional challenges to the scores. This can be positive if it results in an open and fair evaluation of the documentation produced by the product managers. In which case, the selection becomes more impartial and the integrity of the process improves.

5.6.7   Selection Criteria and Weights

The number of section criteria should be kept to less than 5 or 6.

If there are too many selection criteria, they should be combined. For example, if a there is an existing criterion called *Attractive Market*, there is no need to add one called *Health Care*. One simply allocates higher scores for the *Attractive Market* criterion when the product is targeted to health care.

Discussions about which selection criteria to include, and their weights, often bog down, both in class and in companies. When that happens, it is useful for the instructor to point out that, initially, one can only guess at the selection criteria and weights based on the company's desired goals. Over time, as actual data on product success and failure accumulates, both the selection criteria and the weights can be calibrated and adjusted to improve the forecasting of successful products.

After the selection matrix is completed, it should be analyzed for reasonableness. If the matrix results in a plausible order of importance for the products, this helps to validate the selection criteria and their weights. If the group is not comfortable with the order then they can re-evaluate the selection criteria, the weights, and the scores until a reasonable priority order is reached.

It is important for the students to understand that the *selection matrix* does not have the certainty of a mathematical proof. It is a method designed to help predict the future and there are inherent uncertainties in such a process. This emphasizes the importance of a sensitivity analysis, which validates the reasonableness of the selection criteria, their weights, and the assigned scores.

Sometimes, one particular selection criterion results in scores that are very similar for most projects, which indicates that it is not really an effective selection criterion. In which case, it can be removed from the *selection matrix*, which also has the advantage of simplifying the process.

When one selection criterion has scores very similar to another criterion, it indicates that they are doing the same job. In such cases, the students should be encouraged to determine if it is possible to combine criteria, which, again, simplifies the process.

There is no single, correct approach to assigning selection criteria and instructors should be prepared for a diversity of resulting portfolios. The key is for the students to be able to justify precisely why their portfolio makes sense.

It has even been suggested that all weights should be the same because of the "halo effect." This occurs when a product that scores high in one criterion tends to score high in the others.[27]

We believe that Cooper's research establishes that certain critical success factors (CSFs), which are the basis for the selection criteria, are more important than others. Cooper demonstrates that the single most important CSF is a *unique, differentiated product*, which, in turn, means that it should be the highest weighted selection criterion. The next CSF in importance is an *attractive market* and the research shows that, while important, it is not quite as important as the *unique* CSF. Therefore, the weight for *attractive market* should be high, but slightly less than that of *unique.*

Finally, Cooper effectively proves that financial methods are poor at selecting successful products. [1] Financial selection criteria, therefore, should be the lowest weighted. A major reason for poor performance of financial selection criteria is that, in the early stages of product development, it is very difficult to forecast sales, income, and profitability. Such forecasts become even more difficult when the product definition is uncertain and the future time scale increases.

Students often find it hard to ignore the finances and, as a result, tend to rank the financial criteria, such as *Return on Investment*, with an over-inflated weight. This tendency can be counteracted with reminders about the research and a modest

[27]See Rosenzweig. [4] We appear not to have made much progress on the issue. It goes back to Thorndike (1920). [5]

sensitivity analysis, which will quickly determine if the financial criteria are appropriately weighted.

In a company, historical data can be collected and analyzed to validate the values assigned to both their selection criteria and their weights. This process is called *calibration* and helps to remove bias, eliminate opinions, and improve the visibility of the process.

The values for the weights can be chosen to enhance the desired strategy, not just fit the past data. For example, since *Bargery Fabrics* has an aging portfolio, their strategy is to move towards innovative products in the health care market. Therefore, they may assign higher weights to selection criteria that include innovative products. That will favor products that support the desired new strategy.

5.6.8 Kill the Dogs

When companies undertake too many projects, the results are often poor, i.e., projects do not meet performance goals and miss deadlines. Nevertheless, companies are often reluctant to kill off poorly performing products. When portfolio management is implemented, one of the first things that tends to happen, is that the committee starts killing off the dogs.[28]

---

[28] This does not always go down well, especially when it is the CEO's pet project.

CHAPTER

6

IN REAL COMPANIES

In this chapter, we present interesting results from several implementations in real companies of *Dynamic Portfolio Management* based on the *Bargery Fabrics Case*.

6.1 Panaz

Back in 2008, Panaz was one of the first textile companies to embrace the Advanced Skills for Advanced Materials (ASAM) program and its Product Portfolio Management (PPM) training course. The authors delivered a training course in PPM at Panaz, the same one that we delivered many times to companies in the North West of England, U.K.

Shortly thereafter, Panaz began completing more collections, ranges, and custom designs, reporting improvements in teamwork and communications, and delivering more products on time with higher quality. As a result, Tony Attard, the founder and CEO of Panaz, became a champion for ASAM and PPM.

In 2015, the authors added dynamic portfolio management capabilities to their PPM course. Coincidentally, Panaz began facing serious challenges with its new product portfolio: new products were too often late; they experienced significant staff losses; and much of the cohesion that the PPM training had brought about was now lacking. In fact, Tony Attard observed that their PPM system was no longer working and that "Panaz needed to re-boot its New Product Development."

Panaz's business model relies on the continuous development of product ranges and custom designs using innovative fabrics, which results in a particularly dynamic portfolio. Therefore, when Tony Attard asked us to conduct an in-company training course, we saw it as an excellent opportunity to trial the new material in Dynamic Portfolio Management (DPM).

For background, we present this description of Panaz from their website:

> Panaz is one of Europe's leading suppliers of high quality decorative fabrics and wall-coverings for the hospitality, health care, and corporate sectors. Panaz focuses on design excellence and differentiation through technical innovation resulting in a diverse and comprehensive range of beautiful, exclusive, and durable fire retardant furnishing fabrics.

> Panaz's internationally acclaimed interior designers have produced an extensive portfolio of hospitality fabrics for guest rooms in hotels, aboard ships, and in lobbies, theatres, casinos, and restaurants.

6.2   Interview with Mike Gibbins

The DPM training course at Panaz took place over two days in September 2015. Mike Gibbins, the Supply Chain Manager, took part in the training and later, after significant staff turnover, was assigned the responsibility for new product development.

In March 2017, eighteen months after the course, we interviewed Mike Gibbins about the impact of the DPM training on Panaz. An edited transcript of the interview is presented below and it documents the remarkable impact on Panaz of the two-day DPM course.

- The number one aspect of the training was that it improved the visibility of the new product development (NPD) process and the improved visibility was a major factor in Panaz's recent improvement.

- The training was good because it changed the culture of the company.
  - It got everyone on board.
  - We started the NPD implementation from zero, so it was time well spent. We had a couple of people leave and this allowed us to easily change the company's structure and add additional staff.

- The importance of portfolio management was enhanced—we were not doing it well—and, so, we devoted additional resources to it.[1]

- In the past, we developed a 12-month plan and the products were often late.

  - Last year, we did 11-12 programs.

  - Every project now has a path in *Microsoft Project*. There are 47 activities, albeit that many of them are fairly minor.

  - This year, so far, 7 out of 9 products were on time. We even delivered two over Christmas.

  - We already have twenty scheduled for 2017-18 and even more for the following year.[2]

  - We create a budget for each project and the Directors now see the value of the plans. They help with prioritization.[3]

  - Everyone now knows that there is a system and we are doing things that enable them to concentrate on the upper level decisions.

  - We publish milestones and we say to everyone, "Here's your chance to contribute." After that, we just go ahead and do the work.[4]

- We realize now that we were not starting the project planning early enough.

  - We now plan at least a year ahead and we already have a few product plans for the year after that, e.g., those with long lead time fabrics.

  - Production was not involved in the process, now they are.

- Initially, people were a bit hostile to the process. We had to win them over by actually making their lives better.[5]

  - The new process supports better decision-making.

  - It draws attention to delays. We found that the delays tended to be in the same areas of the time line.[6]

  - We can focus more on "What is the product?"[7]

  - There must be a commitment to a launch date. Actually, this is of limited value, because it's a guess and things change. But, people still want to know, "What is the launch date?"

- We are now confident in our process:

[1] Reinforcing the idea that companies often fail to appreciate the importance of portfolio management.

[2] This illustrates the breaking down of rigid yearly product evaluation cycles and moving to a more flexible approach.

[3] Notice the involvement of all levels of staff throughout the company.

[4] An example of the empowerment of lower staff members.

[5] Illustrating the idea that portfolio management cannot be ordered into place, it has to be persuasive.

[6] DPM tends to illuminate management deficiencies, which can be addressed—see *reconfiguring*.

[7] Thus improving the product content.

- Unfortunately, the entire process is not visible to everyone because not everyone has access to *Microsoft Project*. Also, some of those that do have *Project* may not have the time to keep up to speed with the information it contains.[8]

- The development team meets weekly to discuss where each product is. No sales people are involved.

- The project status changes in lots of ways: customers, designs, supply chain changes, market forces, company strategy, styles, and fabric performance. One project had 13 different versions of the budget.[9]

- On one project, a supplier failed. You can't predict that.[10]

- The process is dynamic and enables strategic decision-making. Minutes of the weekly meetings are produced, but they do not list what people said, only action items, which are allocated to specific individuals or departments. Minutes are issued less than 24 hours after the meeting ends. Action items that need the CEO's input are in red.[11]

- It took a while for Sales to get fully on board with our new way of doing things.

  - Getting timely input from staff members who are not based in the office can be a problem.[12]

  - Now everyone understands that once a decision is made, we can get on with the planning, which helps us get better results.

  - We can fill in the operational details: fabric validation, marketing activities, and synchronize with production.

- We take a long-term view and look twelve months ahead:

  - We produce a roadmap with the project list.

  - The roadmap contains all projects for next year.[13]

  - The roadmap even contains some projects in the year after, e.g., those with long lead items, long-term strategic products, and high budget items.

  - The roadmap combines the Budget, Production Schedule, and Marketing Activities.[14]

  - The roadmap generates better plans, it doesn't bunch up milestones. Therefore, we have better, more reasonable production schedules.

[8]DPM is always a work in progress.

[9]Illustrating the *dynamic* nature of Panaz's portfolio

[10]Illustrating unavoidable, dynamic uncertainties in the portfolio.

[11]Illustrating that DPM can be efficient, it need not be bureaucratic.

[12]Each implementation of DPM is unique. Panaz needed to allow access to data by the staff while traveling.

[13]DPM must include all products, which appear on the roadmap–see section 5.6.2.

[14]Showing that the roadmap integrates, and makes visible, activities across the company.

58

- We have a scoping meeting monthly, it usually takes an afternoon and includes the Design Department. Everything goes into the scoping meeting: all design ideas, changes to suppliers, fabric ideas.[15]

• We still have several stumbling blocks that we are working to overcome:

- The main difficulty used to be fabric selection. For example, we might not have an agreement from Sales on a design. Now we get these decisions earlier.

- Sales and Marketing now have a better handle on the process.[16]

- The Design Department can now see the priorities.

- The process is evolving. There used to be tension between Design and Production. Designers tend to want to keep tweaking their work and production people want to get on with making things.[17]

- The process helps us to see what dates and decisions are critical. It gives us visibility.

- Improved visibility is a major factor in our recent improvement.

• We do not wait around anymore:

- We changed the system. We used to require a formal business case to be submitted and to be signed off before anything became a product. Now we get everything in our pipeline with dates, even speculative products, as soon as we are aware of a new product's existence. This means that we put speculative products in with dates.[18]

- 35% of next year's products are not really planned yet, but it gives us a start on them and they are visible.[19]

- Any idea goes into the plan immediately, otherwise we found that the dates were retrospective.

- We've learned that the critical dates are Executive Decisions and Design Decisions. Senior management are now aware of their impact on the schedule.

- We developed a schedule template in *Microsoft Project* that is now used for all products. When a product is proposed, the template is immediately invoked with preliminary dates filled in as much as possible.

- This gives us a general schedule, which we can tailor to Trade Shows, Exhibitions, and Product Launches. All these require finished products. The schedule is dynamic because of these real-world events.[20]

[15] Everything goes into the portfolio.

[16] Illustrating the *reconfiguring* process.

[17] This is typical of design departments, who often cause delays in an attempt to create a perfect product. The roadmap shows the impact of such delays.

[18] Another example of the *reconfiguring* process.

[19] Another example of the DPM process making all products visible.

[20] This illustrates the importance of multiple product deliverables.

59

- We are actually doing more.[21]

    - We will do 17–20 next year.

    - The Supply Chain is more efficient. We can see where we can add value, e.g., we can insert a standard product for a custom design and we can see where we can sell multiple versions of a product.[22]

- We should probably re-do the training every two years.

    - This relates mostly to *Microsoft Project*, but, in more general terms, we need to make sure that new team members have the same understanding of the system as the existing staff.[23]

    - Staff turnover is a problem because, when someone leaves, they take their knowledge with them.

    - Also, if existing staff train new team members, it's difficult to get the new employee to the same level of understanding as the rest of the team.

- The CEO's job is to continually challenge us to do better all the time. He acknowledges that we have improved, but he wants us to find ways to make the process even better and faster.

- The scoping meetings work well and they have improved communication significantly. They also help to manage the team's expectations.

- We have moved massively.

    - We spent time re-designing the portfolio evaluation process and it is much better: It's quicker.[24]

    - We have much clearer information.

    - A few of our products were really quick to market.[25]

    - We linked New Product Development to the Supply Chain.

    - The development of new ranges increases sales, but there is a lag between launch and uptake. Sometimes a range can take 6-18 months to gain momentum. Launching projects on time starts that period sooner rather than later.[26]

    - The NPD Department has added significant value to the business over the last two years with a growth in new ranges and a growth of 30% per year on custom projects.

[21] Dynamic Portfolio Management works.

[22] This shows how DPM makes visible the wider impact of the Supply Chain department—another example of *transforming*.

[23] DPM requires continuous staff development.

[24] Another example of *transforming*; here the re-design of business processes.

[25] An example of the improvement that can accrue from DPM.

[26] Earlier sales revenue from DPM.

- Re-engineering, re-sourcing and innovation all delivered cost and performance improvements.

- We added 3 people to the NPD staff.

- This continues to develop as a relatively new team learns to use the new tools in place to work effectively.

- We have much closer and clearer relations between all departments.

  - Business Development Managers are learning the process and realizing that we can do things faster. They used to ask random, vague questions. Now, they are much better at asking for the right information.

  - I think the process helps the directors to make better decisions. Their decision points are visible and they can understand the consequences better.

  - Tony Attard likes the data, he actually reads everything. His job is to challenge us and he does.[27]

  - Customers are seeing results. We're offering more products, faster. We are delivering on time.

- It's still a work in progress.

  - We don't need to make major changes, but we will continue to make some tweaks along the way.

  - The Design Department is now more involved. We can't make the plans work without them and they are becoming better at giving us specific dates.

  - Our communications still need work.

6.3 The *Nano* Project

We have stated on several occasions that one of the valuable characteristics of DPM is that it is an open process that communicates strategic priorities throughout the company. The following anecdote illustrates the value of an open DPM process.

Several years ago, as part of our work with the U.S. National Textile Center, we were members of the portfolio management committee. The committee's role was to evaluate research proposals submitted by faculty from the consortium's universities and to select the best research and development (R&D) projects.

[27]A significant involvement and a genuine commitment of senior management is critical to the success of DPM.

One year, we had just completed the selection matrix and assigned the budget. We had picked the best projects and were almost done.

The *Nano* project was at the bottom of the selection matrix and the committee was in unanimous agreement that it was poorly conceived and should not be funded. Then, out of the blue, one committee member pointed to the *Nano* project and proposed that the National Textile Center really should invest in nano-technology as a strategic objective. The committee member went on to suggest that, despite its low scores, the *Nano* project should be funded as a strategically valuable investment.

The rest of the committee loudly objected and pointed out that the *Nano* project had unclear benefits and that there were excellent reasons for it being on the bottom of the list. Nevertheless, the committee member persisted and defended the idea that the *Nano* project was *strategically* important and should be funded.

After much heated debate, the committee gradually came to accept the value of an investment in nano-technology. They relented and even moved the *Nano* project to the top of the funding list.

"If it doesn't improve, we can always cancel it next year," the committee member added.

When the list of funded projects was announced, the inclusion of the *Nano* project was greeted with disbelief and confusion by faculty throughout the consortium. Not only within the committee, but among the faculty, there seemed to be general agreement that the *Nano* project was poorly conceived.

Eventually, the uproar died down and faculty began to realize that funding the *Nano* project was a strategically important signal. Faculty began developing nano projects, but realized that they were starting behind the funded *Nano* project. They would have to be even better than the *Nano* project by the time the next funding cycle came around.

One year later, at the next funding cycle meeting, the previous prediction of the portfolio management committee came to pass.

A year later, the *Nano* project was still poorly conceived with unclear benefits. On the other hand, faculty members everywhere were now aware of the strategic importance of nano-technology and proposed several excellent, innovative nano-technology projects. The first *Nano* project was indeed canceled and several new nano projects funded.

While somewhat extreme, this example demonstrates the value of openness in the portfolio management process. It illustrates how strategic goals are communicated by the public selection of projects. It might be argued that a better way to accomplish the same goal would have been to announce that nano-technology was a strategic priority. However, that did not become clear to the portfolio management committee until the *Nano* project was proposed. The faculty member who proposed the *Nano* project was ahead of his colleagues but, unfortunately, with a poor project.

This example also illustrates the interesting relation between individual and collective creativity. Individuals often originate ideas (e.g., the *Nano* project), while companies and universities tend to react to creative ideas. The *Dynamic Portfolio Management* process takes advantage of individual creativity by soliciting product ideas. These product ideas are combined with organizational strategy to maximize the benefits.

6.4   The Empowerment Problem

Training a company's staff in DPM can shake up the traditional power structure by empowering lower-level staff members.

Training in DPM teaches a company's staff to appreciate the critical factors essential for new product success and they come to understand how to evaluate their own company's products against the criteria they establish. In particular, they understand the significance of unique products in attractive markets and begin to feel comfortable selecting which ones the company should invest in and, more significantly, why.

Another frequent occurrence is the killing of projects by the portfolio committee. The committee typically understands the selection rationale and is comfortable with the decision to cancel projects. Often, their work is rewarded when they begin to see the positive results of their work throughout their company.

At this point, we've frequently seen a senior executive interfere in the process. The executive acknowledges the excellent work by the portfolio management team, but then makes unilateral changes to the portfolio. After all, executives are quite used to doing things their own way.

The problem can become serious when a senior executive promotes a product that is neither unique nor in an attractive market. The team quickly jumps to the conclusion that the executive doesn't understand portfolio management.[28]

It is particularly demoralizing when executives ignore the *unique product* critical success factor because the research is so clear on its importance and committee members may be beginning to appreciate its positive impact on the portfolio.

[28]And they are often correct.

It is not unusual for the team to be able to explain just how important product uniqueness is, only to have their work overruled by senior management. Senior managers have empowered the team, praised their work, and then disempowered them with their heavy-handed actions. We have seen this conflict occur frequently in different degrees of seriousness.[29]

In one particular company, a senior executive consistently overruled the committee. After several months of being ignored, most of the portfolio management committee quit. They felt they understood the fundamentals of portfolio management and that the executive was selecting bad products and for obviously wrong reasons. The result was the company lost valuable, senior staff.

On the other hand, many senior executives realize the importance of portfolio management and adjust their approach, becoming an integral part of the process. A positive supporting role is essential, along with establishing a clear company strategy.

To help defuse this issue, Mike Bentley came up with the idea of arranging a meeting with learners and directors a week prior to commencing DPM training. These are referred to as 'scoping' sessions. A key element of these scoping sessions is to match the business drivers, particularly the strategic objectives, with the personal needs of the individual learners. A parallel goal is to evaluate the senior executive's management style and to begin to prepare them for an empowered team.

After the training, Mike informally monitors the actions of the portfolio management team and conducts formal, follow-up interviews with senior executives. By validating, reinforcing, and explaining the team's actions, Mike educates senior executives in the fundamentals of portfolio management and helps to prepare them for the specific changes that are occurring in the company.

Mike's scoping sessions have defused several potential conflicts between empowered teams and senior management.

6.5   Monitoring the Portfolio

Once DPM is in place, a useful follow-on is for the company to develop metrics to assess the performance of the portfolio. At this point it is important to distinguish between the projects and the portfolio. Doing a project well (delivering it on time and on budget) is no guarantee that it contributes to the company's strategy.

[29] In fact, the Chadwick Award (see Acknowledgments) was granted to study just this issue.

Companies desire to measure how the portfolio contributes to the bottom line, which can be difficult to measure. For example, consider the question, *Did the new DPM increase sales?* Any number of events that had nothing to do with the portfolio could have increased sales, e.g., the acquisition of a new customer or the hiring of a new sales person. Therefore, the evaluation of the portfolio must be done with some care.

The following questions can help to assess the portfolio:

- How many customer requirements/needs were met?

- Was there an increase in revenue?

- Was there an expansion of markets?

- Were there cost reductions?

- Was there a change in NPV/ROI?

- Were cycle times are reduced?

At the end of all of the above questions, we should add the phrase "attributable to the portfolio." These questions may be difficult to answer and a qualitative assessment of progress may have to suffice.

Rosenstock has a useful summary of portfolio analysis tools and techniques. [6] While the paper has been around for a while, it is a useful starting point.

7

TEACHING NOTE

The motivation for the case and the general pedagogical approach are presented in this Teaching Note, which provides guidance to instructors in the running of the *Bargery Fabrics* case, both in the classroom and in companies. While the identical content can be used in both environments, the preparation of the students and the pedagogical approaches are slightly different.

A brief overview of the relevant research, and associated theoretical topics, are covered in Chapter 8, Research.

Since we have run this case many times, in both classroom and company environments, we know that the goals and objectives are achievable. Both students in classes and learners in companies regularly complete the assignments within the allocated time frames.

The *Bargery Fabrics* case covers a critically important topic for which there are few practical cases for students and company learners to work through. The case is quite sophisticated and, before the publication of this volume, training in the running of the *Bargery Fabrics* case could only be accomplished by having an experienced trainer or faculty member team-teach the case with someone wishing to learn how to present it.

The goal of this publication, in this extended format, is to provide sufficient information for instructors to be able to present the case from reading and practicing with this book. This goal is supported by the following information:

- Side footnotes[1] throughout the case provide immediate contextual information to the instructor. For example, the significance of the word, "aging," when referring to the *Bargery Fabrics* products might be missed on a casual reading. The side footnote highlights that *Bargery Fabrics'* aging products need to be replaced with innovative products.

- There is not a single solution to the case, although there are preferred approaches. Multiple solutions are provided for the assignments, including several variations that students tend to develop. For each assignment, the key issues are discussed, particularly those that students often fail to appreciate properly. See chapter 5, Answers.

- We provide explicit links between the theoretically important concepts and the practical solution.

- Questions for the instructor are provided for each assignment. These help to focus the students on the critical issues and help them to reach a satisfactory solution.

- For each assignment, we provide guidance for its completion and highlight where the instructor's problems are likely to arise, both with the appreciation of the technical content and with staying on schedule.

7.1 Synopsis

The formal *Synopsis* was presented on page xix.

7.2 Key Issues

The goal is to teach students in classes and learners in companies how to build a portfolio and this is accomplished by putting them in the position of selecting a range of products to form a coherent a portfolio that reflects the company's strategy. Then, taking on the role of advisers to senior management, the students present the case for their portfolio. The skills involved are useful as many companies are poor at creating and managing a portfolio.

Knowledge about the applicable theoretical concepts is required. First and foremost is the idea that the most important critical success factor for a new product is that it must be unique and differentiated. Also, the uniqueness characteristic is evaluated from the customer's perspective, which immediately emphasizes the role of marketing.

[1]This is a side footnote highlighting that side footnotes provide immediate, contextual information.

The next most important idea is that products must be aimed at an attractive market, which is one where there is significant potential income and little competition. Several, less important factors must be considered, such as strategy, risk, innovation, and financial considerations.

The key *skills* that the students acquire are: the ability to create and populate a selection matrix; to allocate research funds to the best products; to analyze the portfolio for dynamic changes; to develop a roadmap that schedules the future development of the selected products; and to present their strategy to upper management.

7.2.1 Why Dynamic Portfolio Management?

In the United States, new products account for about 50% of a company's sales and 40% of their profits. [1] On the other hand, one-third of all new product launches fail and, despite low success rates, companies are reluctant to kill off the poor performers.

Many companies have a mix of products under development, including innovative products, extensions of existing lines, technology investments, and strategic corporate initiatives. In such a complex, dynamic environment, how does a company prioritize and invest in an appropriate mix of products?

Fortunately, research suggests a surprisingly straightforward answer, which is usually referred to as New Product Development (NPD) or Product Portfolio Management (PPM). Once the products' critical success factors are linked to the company's strategic goals, a business process can be implemented that is both easy-to-understand and effective.

Recent research has shown that real-world portfolios are dynamic and must adapt to both internal and external influences. Internally, the products must react to evolving customer demands, different rates of project progress, and revised marketing priorities. Externally, the portfolio must react to the dynamic business environment, which includes corporate strategic initiatives, market changes, as well as technological and social forces.

Therefore, we have added Dynamic Portfolio Management (DPM) to the traditional Product Portfolio Management (PPM).

7.2.2 Why the *Bargery Fabrics* Case?

There is considerable research literature on the methods and tools of portfolio management and their effectiveness in companies is well documented. [1] However, there are few cases available for teaching its practical implementation.

This dearth of cases is entirely understandable. Companies regard their data on successful new products as highly sensitive and successful strategies are a competitive weapon. Companies are, therefore, reluctant to publish their data or their hard-won experiences. This deficiency was a significant motivation for developing a practical case for teaching portfolio management.

When teaching of portfolio management in companies, an important early activity is an honest evaluation of the company's historical projects, both successes and failures. It is not unusual to find that many in the audience were involved in previous projects and a dialog about their successes and failures exposes sensitivities and often results in uncomfortable discussions.

We quickly learned, therefore, that beginning the teaching of portfolio management by evaluating a company's successes and failures did not work well because emotions clouded an honest assessment of the company's products and hindered the learning of key new concepts. To defuse this issue, we developed the *Bargery Fabrics Case*, which we now run on the first day of a two-day training session.

After completing the *Bargery Fabrics Case* on day #1, the identical process is repeated on day #2, but using the company's own products. When the *Bargery Fabrics* case is covered first, the trainees typically arrive on Day #2 excited to apply their new found skills to their own products and the assignments proceed smoothly.

While it may appear that starting with the *Bargery Fabrics Case* extends the training, the overall results are much improved. The appreciation of the theoretical concepts is enriched and the students acquire a much better understanding of why their company's products succeeded or failed. In particular, product failures are often associated with a lack of uniqueness, the most important Critical Success Factor (CSF). Presenting the *Bargery Fabrics Case* removes the personal defensiveness and replaces it with an independent, unbiased assessment in terms of the CSFs.[2]

After several successful implementations in companies, the *Bargery Fabrics Case*, was adapted to the classroom and became a regular component of a graduate course in Project Management. Students obtain an understanding of the concepts of portfolio management, which is an important aspect of Project Management.

[2] See the experiences in Chapter 6, In Real Companies.

7.3 Target Audiences

There are two target audiences for the *Bargery Fabrics* case and, without changes, has been used successfully with both target audiences:

- *Companies wishing to introduce, or upgrade, their portfolio management.*

  Typically, senior executives sense a need for improvement in their portfolio management and request a training course. Running the case in a company is usually referred to as "training" and is typically part of a two-day course in *Dynamic Portfolio Management*. The training is most effective when the learners represent critical departments throughout the company.

- *Graduate students in Project Management.*

  Since project selection is one of the first topics in the project life cycle, the *Bargery Fabrics Case* is an interesting and effective exercise early in a Project Management (PM) course. PM graduate students are typically mid-career professionals with business experience. They are often "accidental" project managers, i.e., they find themselves working on projects with no formal training in the discipline.

  The time devoted to the case depends on the priority assigned to the topic of *project selection*. We believe that this is an important topic because company capabilities are generally poor in this area. Therefore, it is valuable for project management students to learn the skills of *Dynamic Portfolio Management*.

The authors have not tested this case with undergraduates because we believe that the case requires experience in real world product development, which undergraduates lack. Also, we do not teach undergraduates, our teaching experience is only with working professionals.

The same *Bargery Fabrics Case* can be used for both target audiences. The differences are in the implementation schedule and the preparation of the students. The plan for teaching an academic, project management course is covered in section 7.5 and the plan for an in-company training course is covered in section 7.6.

7.4 Learning Outcomes

There are two sets of learning outcomes from the *Bargery Fabrics Case*. The first includes the demonstration of the *technical* skills required to assess the portfolio:

71

creating the critical success factors, completing the selection matrix, and developing the roadmap. The second set of learning outcomes requires *analytical* skills: assessing the dynamic contributions to the portfolio, and presenting a list of products consistent with the articulated *Bargery Fabrics* strategy.

These learning outcomes establish that the students have mastered the vocabulary, the technical competencies, and the analytical skills necessary to develop a new product portfolio. Since these capabilities are often missing from companies, they are valuable real-world skills.

The formal learning outcomes are:

1. Using portfolio management concepts, students will develop a list of critical success factors, complete the selection matrix, and derive the roadmap.

2. Students will apply dynamic portfolio management concepts and write a presentation that makes recommendations for a coherent portfolio of new products consistent with the articulated company strategy.

7.4.1 Skills

To educate the students in portfolio management, the case develops specific skills through a coordinated set of lectures and workshops designed to help them master:

- The formal concepts underlying the development of a potentially successful portfolio of new products: critical success factors, the important link between the technical and marketing issues, and dealing with the dynamic nature of portfolios.

- The evaluation of a wide selection of products with realistic characteristics that reflect the challenges and diversity found in real world products.

- The tools to evaluate the potential future commercial success of products, such as the product selection matrix and the roadmap.

- The development and presentation of a coherent product roadmap, which is consistent with the company's articulated strategy.

The goal of the case is to develop a coherent product development strategy for *Bargery Fabrics*, which requires the following steps:

- Study the information about *Bargery Fabrics* in Chapter 1. Asses their articulated strategy with regard to their proposed new products.

- Develop the critical success factors, applicable to *Bargery Fabrics*, for the evaluation of their new products.[3]

- Develop the selection matrix, which scores the new products, and present a rationale for which ones should be implemented.

- Allocate the development budget to the best products.

- Assess the dynamic aspects of the portfolio and develop a product roadmap for the implementation of *Bargery Fabrics'* products.

- Present the entire strategy to upper management.

7.5 Classroom Teaching Strategy

7.5.1 The Graduate Student Audience

We have successfully run the *Bargery Fabrics Case* many times in a single 3-hour class of graduate Project Management students. While the case itself can be completed in one class, the students need to come to class prepared and this can be accomplished by delivering a lecture on *Dynamic Portfolio Management* the week before.

The assignments should be completed in teams because it is valuable for them to present their results to the other teams to compare and discuss approaches. However, the discussions take longer, and the issues tend to repeat, when there are more than about 25-30 students. In that case, it is effective to alternate the team presentations for different assignments.

In the final assignment, students present their roadmap and propose a product strategy. This is a critical skill that demonstrates the students have learned the essential skills of *Dynamic Portfolio Management*. It is particularly valuable to have multiple teams present their strategies and to critically analyze their approaches. Therefore, it is important for the instructor to keep the case moving so that there is time for this final assignment.

There is no single right answer and the instructor should, if possible, encourage the teams to pursue different approaches, which results in more interesting discussions. The instructor should also emphasize that each team must justify their approach based on the data in the case, not on random, or preconceived, opinions.

[3]Unique, differentiated products; attractive markets; effective launches.

7.5.2 Graduate Student Preparation

In the week before the case is to be run, we typically present a lecture on the fundamental concepts of portfolio management that covers the critical success factors, the selection matrix, the roadmap, and the dynamic evaluation of the portfolio. Also, the students are assigned two homework tasks:

1. Read the *Bargery Fabrics Case.*

2. Develop a preliminary list of Critical Success Factors (CSFs).

The students are then familiar with the details of the case and prepared to begin work on the case immediately. In class, the students are placed in teams and, with their preparation of the selection criteria, they can proceed quickly to the assignments.

Students should be encouraged to bring laptops to class. This speeds up the completion of the selection matrix, which is the most time-consuming exercise.

7.5.3 Exam Question

The following question has been used in a two-hour mid-term exam. The question is designed to take about a half hour to complete.

The question covers the essential theoretical ideas from *Dynamic Portfolio Management* in a relatively simple problem. Developing the selection criteria, their weights, and filling out the selection matrix ensures that the students can perform the key technical aspects of portfolio management. (Learning Outcome #1.)

The last part of the question ensures that the students can analyze and apply the concepts of *Dynamic Portfolio Management* and make recommendations for a coherent portfolio consistent with the articulated company strategy. (Learning Outcome #2.)

Question: Select a New Personal Car

1. Choose four selection criteria, based on the critical success factors (CSFs), that are important to you in the selection of a car. Explain why the criteria represent features that are important to you.

2. Assign weights to the selection criteria and briefly explain why you assigned those values.

3. Select some *previous* cars with which you have experience (yours, friends', parents', relatives', etc.). Explain why they are relevant to the decision to buy your new car.

4. Fill out the selection matrix for the *previous* cars using your selection criteria and weights.

5. How would you proceed from here in the selection of a new car that satisfies your needs?

6. What are some of the issues involved?

Typical Answer:

1. I chose the following four selection criteria that are important to me in the selection of a car.

   - Safety: Most important to me.

   - Reliability: I don't want to lose time with the car in the shop.

   - Low Cost: I'm on a student budget.

   - Sporty: That is my preferred style.

2. I assigned the following weights to the selection criteria.

   - Safety (5). Most important.

   - Reliability. (4) My time is important.

   - Low Cost (4). I'm on a student budget.

   - Sporty (2). That's my preferred style, but this is less important than the other factors.

3. I picked a variety of different types of cars to spread the scores out, to validate my selection process, and to make an effective calibration. I also picked cars I knew something about, so that I could score them accurately.

   At this point, I analyzed the table to determine if the cars with the highest scores were the cars that meet my established goals. For example, Mom's SUV has the highest score, which was determined because of its high scores in safety and reliability. Therefore, these selection criteria dominate the scores.

Table 7.1: Selection Matrix for my cars.

Vehicle	Safety (5)	Reliability (4)	Low Cost (4)	Sporty (2)	Total Score
Dad's Sedan	8	6	7	5	86
Friend's Compact	6	7	9	7	108
Mom's SUV	9	9	6	4	113
Uncle's Luxury	9	9	1	6	97

Mom's SUV has the highest score and I have to decide if it represents the type of car that I want. This is the strategy step in which I determine if I am comfortable with the final selection. I am happy with Mom's SUV as my choice.

4. From here, I would proceed as follows:

The first step is to determine if my table is reasonable. The selection criteria were proposed in Question #1 and that defined my strategy, e.g. safety was most important to me, followed by maintenance free.

This completes the calibration step, which validates the selection criteria, the weights, and the scores.

From here I would select several cars that I might want to purchase in the future. I would repeat the process and score the new cars using the weights and criteria I established above.

5. The issues:

- The best cars are not always at the top. Therefore, I analyzed the scores to see if the results make sense. I noted that the total scores for my Friends Compact and Mom's SUV are similar, so I examined the scores. Maybe the Compact is not as safe as the SUV and, so, I revised the safety score down slightly to 6.

- All cars have similar safety scores and, therefore, the selection process tended to be dominated by the Reliability and the Cost. My Uncle's Luxury was eliminated by the cost criterion.

7.6   Company Teaching Strategy

In companies, this case is designed to be completed in a series of interleaved brief seminars and workshops. This breaks up the lecturing component, which is particularly desirable in a commercial environment where the learners are less likely to be familiar with conventional lectures.

A complication is that company learners frequently show up without having read the case. Therefore, a reasonable approach is to quickly cover the essential ideas in short, mini-lectures to give the learners a working vocabulary. Then, as quickly as reasonable, place them in teams and proceed to the assignments in workshops, where the skills are implemented and the vocabulary reinforced.

In companies, we typically teach *Dynamic Portfolio Management* in a two-day training course. Table 7.2 shows a typical schedule for training in companies.

During Day #1 we cover the *Bargery Fabrics Case* and begin with the concepts and implementation methods of classic *Product Portfolio Management* (PPM). During the afternoon of Day #1, we cover the concepts and implementation methods of *Dynamic Portfolio Management* (DPM).

Before coming to the second day's training session, learners should be encouraged to think about their own company's products. They should bring a list of a dozen or so of their company's products, including interesting, new and old, successes and failures. This is useful preparation and allows them to think about what made the products successful, or not, in terms of the concepts and vocabulary they acquired on Day #1, e.g., which company products were unique and differentiated? Which were launched into attractive markets?

During Day #2, we cover the same materials as in Day #1, but using the company's own products. On Day #2 learners are prepared to evaluate their own products honestly and realistically employing concepts and vocabulary learned on Day #1. On Day #2, learners often appreciate the *reasons* for a particular product's failure and, frequently, that it was neither unique nor differentiated. Day #2 usually ends with the entire group presenting their newly developed product strategy for the company to upper management.

Even when the goal is to provide company-specific training in the development of a unique portfolio, it is valuable to complete the *Bargery Fabrics Case* first. Working through the case educates employees in the vocabulary, techniques, and processes in a non-confrontational situation. Thus, we refer to the Day #1, where we run the *Bargery Fabrics* case, as "PPM detox."

We have not done it, but it is conceivable that the case could also be offered in 2-3 separate modules over time to accommodate busy employee schedules.

The *Bargery Fabrics* case is particularly effective when there are at least two teams presenting their results and this is true even if the teams are small (3-4 people in each team). We have found that training six people in two teams of three is much more effective than training a single team of six. There are multiple successful strategies and presenting competing approaches continually forces the learners to justify their approach based on data, not on personal opinion.

Follow-on training sessions can be conducted at the company site to help embed the concepts in the company by using the company's actual, historical and future products and the associated company data. This is an additional effort that is not described here.

7.6.1 Company Learner Preparation

Company learners should be encouraged to read the case before attending the session. However, on several occasions, we have shown up at a company and the trainees have not even read the case. The disadvantage is that it takes a little longer to explain the important concepts before the assignments can be started. On the other hand, company trainees usually have a background in product development and tend to pick up the theoretical concepts quite quickly. Placing the trainees in groups early on creates a team environment that helps to overcome the lack of preparation.

After the completion of each assignment, the teams should present their results to the other teams. This encourages discussion, reinforces the vocabulary and critical concepts, and requires each team to back up their opinions with data from the case.

Learners should be encouraged to bring laptops to the training sessions, which speeds up the completion of the selection matrix, the most time-consuming exercise. Also, today's learners are usually familiar with presentation tools and the final assignment—present the strategy to upper management—can be effectively delivered using spreadsheets and presentation tools.

7.6.2 Company Training Plan

An outline of the content for a typical one-day company training session in the *Bargery Fabrics Case* is shown in Table 7.2.

7.7 The Assignments

The pedagogical aspects of completing the assignments were covered in chapter 5, Answers. The *Bargery Fabrics Case* is designed to take the students gradually through the assignments, which are completed in discrete, manageable steps.

Table 7.2: Outline of a *Bargery Fabrics Case* training session.

Time	Topic	Activity
09:00	Introduction Aims & Objectives	Discussion: Importance of New Product Development
09:30	Portfolio Management Critical Success Factors	Workshop: Create Selection Criteria for *Bargery Fabrics*
10:15	Break	
10:30	Portfolio Selection Matrix	Workshop: Develop the Selection Matrix for *Bargery Fabrics*
12:00	Lunch	
12:30	Selecting the Best Products The Budget	Workshop: Analyze selected products Allocate budget
13:30	Product Selection Strategy	Workshop: Propose product strategy
14:00	Dynamic PPM Internal Portfolio Changes	Workshop: Develop preliminary roadmap
15:00	Break	
15:30	Dynamic PPM External Portfolio Changes	Workshop: Develop final roadmap
16:30	Lessons Learned	Discussion: Does the portfolio reflect *Bargery Fabrics'* strategy?

Each assignment is designed to deliver a specific result and to reinforce a key concept or skill in portfolio management.

7.8 The Bargery Fabrics Product List

When we were developing the case, we interviewed several companies who agreed to provide portfolio data. From the interviews, we established a set of issues that we believed would be both important and useful when learning portfolio management. These issues included: the explicit link to strategically important products; support for long-term, high-risk investments; the synergy between multiple products using the same technology platform; complex products with incremental releases over time; products with multiple market spaces; the potentially negative cost impact of licensing another company's technology; and the market disincentives of commodity products.

However, most companies only face a few of the above issues. Therefore, we modified and combined products from a number of companies to create a coherent product set for our mythical *Bargery Fabrics* company.

Also, many companies face compliance projects, which are required by regulatory updates, information technology upgrades, tax and environmental law changes, etc. Compliance projects compete for funds and should be included in the portfolio process. However, the scenario only requires one such product to make it clear how to handle such compliance projects and the *Silver Monitoring* product was added to the portfolio.

7.8.1 Anti-Microbial Products

While *Bargery Fabrics'* products are based on *anti-microbial* technology, students do not require any prior knowledge about the technology. The techniques presented in the case are completely general and can used in any company in any industrial sector.

The anti-microbial topic was originally selected for the Advanced Flexible Materials (AFM) business sector. Several advanced manufacturing sectors depend upon anti-microbial technology, which is a significant contributor to the economy in the U.K.

The products were simplified so that the case could be used in a wide variety of industries and in the classroom without any prior knowledge of anti-microbial technology. The anti-microbial technology provides a technical flavor to the products that is necessary to convey an advanced, innovative portfolio. At the same time, the case can be run without requiring any previous knowledge on the part of the students or company learners.

We believe the current set of products is sophisticated enough to make the case realistic while, at the same time, the products and technologies are easily understandable by students and learners with no exposure either to portfolio management or to anti-microbial technologies.

7.9 Miscellaneous Issues

7.9.1 Products vs. Projects

There is a considerable overlap between the fields of *Product* Portfolio Management and *Project* Portfolio Management:

- *Product* Portfolio Management is about selecting the right *products*,

- *Project* Portfolio Management is about selecting the right *projects*.

A *project* is defined as a "unique temporary endeavor." [7] More colloquially, a project is unique, has not been done before, has a beginning and an end, and has established stakeholder requirements. [3] A *product* is a tangible commercial creation and, because uniqueness is such an important factor, developing a *product* is clearly a *project*.

Since products and projects are so closely related, the entire process of *Dynamic Portfolio Management*, as described here, can be used unchanged for the selection of *projects* as well as the selection of *products*. While the names are different, the fundamental techniques are the same.

Therefore, the *Bargery Fabrics Case* can be used unchanged for the teaching of *Project Portfolio Management* and can be taught in a Project Management course.

Program Management is the cooperative management of multiple projects and project selection is usually one of the first topics taught. Therefore, the *Bargery Fabrics Case* is also relevant to the teaching of *Program Management*.

7.9.2 Project Management vs. Portfolio Management

Project Management (PM) is not part of this case, which focuses entirely on the management of the portfolio, i.e., the selection of new products.

A project manager is responsible for delivering agreed content within the assigned budget and schedule. Therefore, the successful development of products clearly requires effective project management.

An important facet of classic PM is the Change Control Board (CCB), whose goal is to control the project's content by managing changes, which are only allowed after a thorough assessment of their impact on performance, cost, and schedule. As such, the CCB's job is often to discourage change.

On the other hand, Petit and Hobbs emphasize that portfolios encounter very high levels of scope changes. [2] For example, they found that only 50% of identified requirements made it into the final project. Therefore, in DPM, a new requirement is not viewed as a change to be discouraged; high-priority requirements should be embraced and implemented, while lower priority requirements will be delayed or removed. Therefore, adding a formal CCB to portfolio management, to decide on which changes to implement, results in significant wasted effort.

Also, DPM tends to delegate the authority over product changes to the product managers, rather than an external CCB. The rationale is that product managers understand best how to trade off between evolving technical content, the budget impact, and the value of the proposed changes to their customers.

Project management is usually centralized in that a single project manager is responsible for the project. DPM, on the other hand is inherently distributed among many departments. Many companies assign a facilitator who organizes processes and reports to management, a role often referred to as a *process engineer*.[4]

Another characteristic of DPM is that the product's budget is fixed. Therefore, classic PM risk management is not employed, i.e., contingency funds and reserves are not allocated. Instead, project content is changed. As a result, projects tend to spend their allocation of funds, but product managers can change the product content to meet customer demands. In DPM, the driver is the content, not the funds.

7.10 Cases vs. Scenarios

The formal definition of a case includes the requirement that it use real data from a real company. The *Bargery Fabrics Case* is made up from a composite of companies and products. Therefore, it is technically more correct to say that *Bargery Fabrics* would generally be considered as a teaching scenario, rather than a teaching case.

---

[4]Mike Gibbins is excellent example of this role, see Chapter 6, In Real Companies.

82

8

RESEARCH

8.1 The Importance of Portfolio Management

The importance of Portfolio Management is established by observing that, in the United States, new products now account for about 50% of companies' sales revenues and 40% of their profits.[1]

Therefore, an important measure of a company's success is its new product success rate, i.e., the proportion of products entering the development stage that eventually become commercial successes. On average, the success rate is a respectable 60%, but there are huge differences between the top performers and average performers: the top 20% of companies have a 20% higher success rate and less than half the failure rate.[2]

On the other hand, companies struggle with portfolio management and, if the research is to be believed, most companies are not very good at it. In fact, only one out of four product development projects succeeds commercially. Cooper suggests that managers offer several possible reasons[3] for why the critical success factors are invisible, for why projects seem to go wrong, for why they take too long, and for why they aren't performed well. [8, 1]

1. *Ignorance*: Companies simply don't know what should be done to make products successful.

[1] Cooper's work validates and emphasizes the importance of new products. [1]

[2] The best companies have an 80% success rate.

[3] Cooper calls them "blockers."

2. *Lack of skills*: Companies don't understand the key drivers of success (the critical success factors) or how to perform key tasks (the market research).

3. *Cross Functional Teams*: DPM involves many departments, all with a significant stake. A single, all-powerful leader will not work. The team requires a genuine commitment of resources.

4. *Faulty processes*: The company's processes don't work. They are missing key elements, they are bureaucratic, and they are incorrectly applied.

5. *Too confident*: Companies think they already know the answers, so why do all the extra work?

6. *Lack of discipline*: Unfortunately, the lack of discipline often starts at the top. Leaders must understand their roles—see section 8.3.4.

7. *Big hurry*: They're in a rush, so they cut corners.

8. *Too many projects*: There are not enough resources, so there's a lack of both money and people to get the job done.

Fortunately, the answer to these deficiencies is a relatively straightforward approach: *Dynamic Portfolio Management*.

We divide the research on portfolio management into three components:

- *Classic Product Portfolio Management (PPM)*.

- *Dynamic Portfolio Management (DPM)*.

- *Blue Ocean and Red Ocean strategies*.

8.2 Classic Product Portfolio Management (PPM)

Classic PPM is well described in Cooper's *Winning at New Products*, which is very readable even by novices in PPM. The research, much of which is Cooper's, has been validated over the past two decades. [1]

According to Cooper, PPM has the following goals: [9]

- Efficient Allocation of Resources.

  Portfolios contain many inter-related factors, such as business objectives, profitability, strategic goals, and synergies between technology platforms.

- Achieving Portfolio Balance

  Portfolios have short and long-term objectives; high risk, innovative and low-risk, income producing products; multiple markets; and multiple technologies.

- Meeting Strategic Objectives.

  Portfolio management is designed to further corporate strategic objectives, rather than meet financial goals, which characterized earlier approaches. This requires managing spending across markets, technologies, and strategic goals. This is often called "strategic alignment."

Cooper's work is fundamental in that it defined the Critical Success Factors (CSFs) for new products. Cooper suggests there are six major factors in the success of new products: [10]

1. Products strategically aligned with corporate objectives.

2. Unique, differentiated products that provide a competitive advantage to the company and value to the customer.

3. Products that compete in an attractive market.

4. Products that build on company strengths and enhance their competitive advantages.

5. Products that are technically feasible and whose risks are managed.

6. Products that produce financial rewards.

In our presentation of the CSFs, we simplify this list by grouping together #1 and #2 as well as #4 and #5. We also emphasize the lower importance of #6, as the research continues to show the reduced effectiveness of using financial methods in product evaluation.[4]

This is justified as Cooper's work established that the most significant CSF is a *unique product*. This was a dramatic discovery and, almost overnight, eliminated much of the conventional thinking about portfolio evaluation, which was traditionally built on financial forecasts.[5]

The next most importance CSF is launch into an *attractive market*, which is defined as one that has significant income potential[6] and little competition.[7]

[4] Predicting future revenue or profitability is difficult at best.

[5] Usually, Return on Investment (ROI).

[6] Otherwise, why do it?

[7] A blue ocean.

85

The CSFs are made specific and combined with the company strategy to form the criteria for the *selection matrix*. The criteria are then weighted, which ties the company strategy to the products. The products are then scored in the *selection matrix*.

The top products in the *selection matrix* are recommended to be funded. However, the matrix must be used with intelligence as individual scores can be challenged and the strategic fit of the selected products debated. A sensitivity analysis helps to mitigate these risks.

When the initial list of products exceeds the proposed research budget, students are often surprised to learn that budgets can be changed and that they can move money around to achieve their strategic goals.[8] Also, company strategy often suggests moving synergistic products into the portfolio and poorly performing products out, e.g., elevating critical products with synergy and killing off poorly performing projects.[9]

8.2.1 Scoring Models

The *selection matrix* is the fundamental tool of Classic PPM. It is a scoring model and falls into the category of "benefits management techniques," which are designed to rely less on the economic data (sales, profitability, etc.) and more on the strategic fit with corporate objectives and market attractiveness. [10, p.16]

Research shows that no single method works in all situations and companies must adapt and tailor the methods to their own particular needs and situation. While no single method works everywhere, scoring models have been validated and proven to be effective tools for portfolio management. [1]

Scoring models can be complemented with other useful tools, such as bubble diagrams, which provide a visual identification of product classes. However, portfolio management is an inherently multi-dimensional problem and two-dimensional representations can over-simplify the process. [10]

Also, since most companies are poor at portfolio management, they need a place to start and scoring models provide enough sophistication without undue burdens of time or difficulty. Once a scoring model has been adapted to a particular company, other tools can be added as needed.

Therefore, we believe that scoring models are an excellent tool for companies to begin implementing portfolio management. Unfortunately, beyond reading about scoring models, there is a dearth of practical exercises that companies can work through before embarking on such important business-changing processes. The *Bargery Fabrics Case* provides a starting point for companies to become familiar with the practical implementation of portfolio management.

[8]Trainees in companies are usually more sanguine, they are quite used to their budgets being cut.

[9]See the discussion of the "Nano" project, section 6.3.

8.2.2   Criticisms of Classic Portfolio Management

The end point of Classic PPM is the *selection matrix*, which is a proposed list of projects to be funded. However, we suggest that, after the completion of the *selection matrix*, there is a need for a portfolio evaluation process in which the selected products are analyzed to ensure that they implement the stated company strategy. Therefore, we have always added a final act to the running of the *Bargery Fabrics Case*: Present an assessment of your proposed portfolio and explain how it meets the strategic goals of the company.

Classic PPM has also been criticized for its inability to handle innovative and dynamic projects. Innovative projects evolve and change in response to customer demands and market forces. PPM provides no formal mechanism to handle such changes.

Finally, in many years of teaching the *Bargery fabrics Case*, we often felt that the final step—the strategic assessment of the portfolio—was poorly supported by research. While it seemed obvious that the portfolio that resulted from the selection matrix should implement and enhance the company's strategy, there was no formal mechanism to accomplish that task.

While Cooper's research supporting the *selection matrix* is solid, evaluating the resulting portfolio for consistency with the company's strategy always seemed, at least to us, somewhat unstructured and *ad hoc*. There was no vocabulary or validated process for approaching such an assessment.

8.2.3   Motivating Dynamic Portfolio Management

The selection-matrix-based PPM process has been accused of being too linear, too rigid, and too bureaucratic. These criticisms are based on the observation that, once the selection matrix is completed, the entire PPM process then runs unchanged until the next product evaluation cycle. Therefore, the process does not allow for evolution in products, business strategy, or markets.

In reality, a portfolio is non-linear, is not cyclical, is discontinuous and is unpredictable. As a result, there is a need to manage variability and uncertainty in personnel, budgets, technology, customers, and product content.

8.3   Dynamic Portfolio Management (DPM)

In 2013, Petit and Hobbs suggested that the selection matrix results in a static view of new products, while real-world portfolios are inherently dynamic. [2] They demonstrated that, in a modern portfolio, it is necessary to adapt to change and uncertainty, and that such dynamism arises both from within and external to the portfolio.

Petit and Hobbs provide a thorough portfolio management literature review along with a comparison of other researchers' definitions, methods, processes, risks and rewards. Petit and Hobbs's research enhances Teece's dynamic framework, which suggests that adapting to change and gaining strategic advantage requires *constant* continual reassessment of the products, and ongoing re-optimization and re-alignment of resources. [11]

Petit and Hobbs demonstrate that organizations see improved performance when they adapt to their environment. Furthermore, they propose processes that are practical and easily implemented.

Portfolio Management has inherently conflicting objectives. Efficiency improves when processes, tools, and techniques remain consistent, which provides stability. However, flexibility is required in adapting the portfolio to uncertainties and changes. A strength of the Petit and Hobbs approach is that it clarifies the distinction between the processes, which need to be stable, and the portfolio content, which is dynamic.

While the Petit and Hobbs research was based on just a few cases in the banking industry, their mechanisms of "sensing, seizing, reconfiguring, and transforming" provide a formal research basis to support the strategic assessment of a dynamic portfolio.

Petit and Hobbs observed that the modern tendency is to deliver multiple, smaller products. The goal is to produce smaller, faster deliveries that are technically feasible and, simultaneously, valuable to the customer. This agrees with Cooper's research by continuing to emphasize the importance of an *attractive market*. Dividing products into multiple deliveries and evaluating their market success requires constant coordination and teamwork between the technical and marketing departments.

For example, Apple now releases new products on a predictable yearly cycle. However, the content of those products is determined by what is technically ready on the scheduled release date. Also, customer feedback is actively solicited in determining the priority of content for subsequent releases.

Therefore, we added the Petit and Hobbs research to Cooper's work in Classic PPM to create *Dynamic Portfolio Management* (DPM). The *Bargery Fabrics Case* was then upgraded to incorporate the features of *Dynamic Portfolio Management*.

To address the above criticisms, Cooper has often been asked, "What is next?" He frequently admits that, for many years, he did not have an answer. Lately, he sees several different approaches emerging from progressive companies. [12]

While not specifically proposing solutions to these criticisms, Cooper has suggested that the next generation of processes should be more agile, vibrant, dynamic, and flexible, while simultaneously being leaner, faster, and more adaptive. [12] Cooper described the requirements for an improved new product development process as the *Triple A* system: it should be adaptive, agile, and accelerated.[10]

- *Adaptive:* The continued emphasis on involving customers early and often through a series of build-test-revise iterations.

- *Agile:* Next-generation systems should also incorporate elements of *Agile Development*, i.e., rapid sprints and scrums and deliverables that can be demonstrated to stakeholders. [13]

- *Accelerated:* Projects require dedicated, cross-functional teams for maximum speed to market.

In Table 8.1, we present Cooper's requirements for future portfolio management along with the characteristics of *Dynamic Portfolio Management.*

8.3.1 Research in Dynamic Portfolio Management

Since the research on DPM is not as accessible as that on traditional PPM, we present here a brief summary of the main points.

Petit and Hobbs defined a set of formal processes necessary for performing a dynamic assessment of the portfolio. Their dynamic assessment addresses several critical defects in Classic PPM:

- It provides a vocabulary that describes the dynamism in the portfolio.

- It adds a new deliverable to the PPM process, the *roadmap*, which is a multi-project plan that describes the delivery of all product content over time.

- It completes Classic PPM by adding formal mechanisms for the continuous strategic assessment of the portfolio.

[10]However, while an excellent start, we feel that his answer is still rather vague.

89

Table 8.1: Cooper's Requirements and DPM Characteristics.

Cooper's *Triple A* Requirements	DPM Characteristics
Adaptive: The continued emphasis on involving customers early and often through a series of build-test-revise iterations.	The Sensing, Seizing, Reconfiguring, and Transforming activities provide a solid research foundation for assessing the dynamic aspects of the portfolio.
Agile: Incorporate elements of *Agile Development*, i.e., rapid sprints and scrums with deliverables that can be demonstrated to stakeholders.	The metaphor of the train schedule is an excellent tool that supports agility. The roadmap encourages multiple, smaller deliveries and, even, a fuzzy definition of their content, which improves communication with customers.
Accelerated: Projects require dedicated, cross-functional teams for maximum speed to market.	The roadmap makes visible the interaction between departments and accelerates the successful deployment of new products.

DPM recognizes that dynamic changes to the portfolio result in uncertainty and turbulence and that these occur both internally, within the portfolio, and externally, from the business environment.

As a result, two sets of activities must be performed: an internal assessment of the portfolio and an external assessment of the company environment. [2] Such dynamism requires *continuous* re-assessment and updating of the portfolio, which must respond to two types of dynamic activities:

Internal Dynamism:

The dynamism in the portfolio's internal, operational aspects leads to internal reconfiguring of the products and their content, e.g., evolving technical requirements, changing customer demands, re-prioritizing funds, canceling projects, etc.

To respond to the internal dynamism, the following activities are pursued:

- *Sensing*: These are the mechanisms to identify and interpret changes within the portfolio.

The most important sensing activity is the identification of customer requirements and their translation into product specifications. Other examples of sensing include identifying new target markets, changing customer needs, evolving technologies, re-distribution of funds, and changing supplier capabilities.

- *Seizing*: These are the mechanisms for deciding on changes within the portfolio, once the need has been sensed.

  User trials are an excellent seizing mechanism in that they help to refine the value of the product's content. Other examples of seizing include selecting: decision-making protocols, customer solutions, and technology platforms. Technology evolution improves the underlying platform resulting in performance improvements. Technology upgrades can improve the product architecture and result in new functionality.

  Petit and Hobbs admit that it is not always easy to distinguish between sensing and seizing.

- *Reconfiguring*: These are the mechanism that result in the reconfiguration of the portfolio.

  Reconfiguring is a continuous re-assessment and re-alignment of the products in the portfolio. This is typically accomplished by adding (or removing) resources (people, funds); dividing products into multiple, smaller deliveries; adding and deleting products; and re-prioritizing products.

The output from the above processes is a preliminary product roadmap, which displays the schedule of key product content deliveries over time.

External Dynamism:

The dynamism in the external business environment leads to transforming of the company processes, e.g., new corporate strategies, the introduction of new processes, the evolution of markets, etc.

To respond to the external dynamism, the following activities are pursued:

- *Sensing*: Mechanisms to identify and interpret changes that affect the business.

- *Seizing*: Mechanisms for *deciding* on changes to the business, once the need has been sensed.

- *Transforming*: The actual reconfiguration of the business.

  Transforming involves higher-level activities and requires embracing innovation. Typical activities include introducing new management structures, developing new skills, re-prioritizing markets, and updating strategy and processes.

The result is the final product roadmap, which displays the schedule of key product content deliveries over time. The above processes are presented as linear, but, in reality, the activities will be mixed up.

8.3.2 The Roadmap

The roadmap is a multi-project plan that shows all known project content deliveries over time. The roadmap shows key content milestones and multiple product releases and typically covers 18-24 months, which immediately extends the view beyond the traditional yearly cycle of PPM.

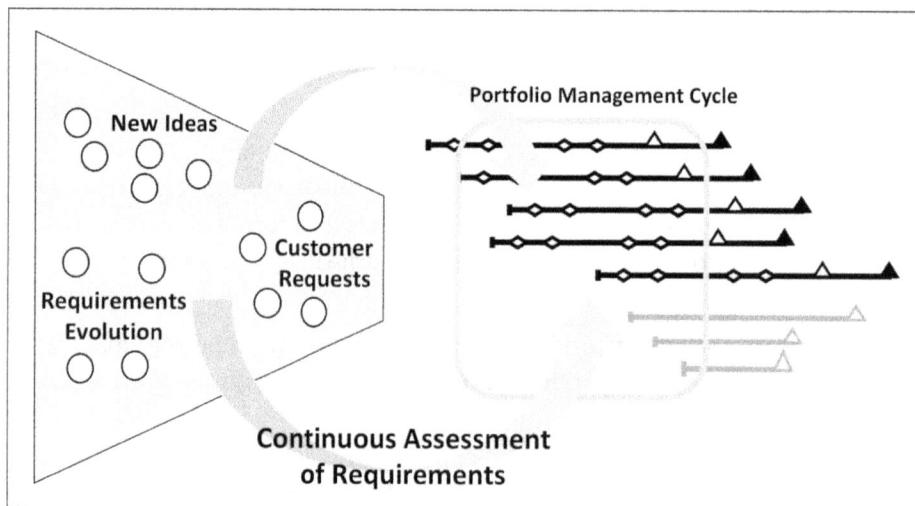

Figure 8.1: The train-schedule metaphor for the roadmap.

The compelling metaphor for the roadmap is a *train schedule*. Train arrival times (the time table) are published and predictable. However, the numbers of coaches, and the content of those coaches, are not predictable.

Like the time table, the roadmap lists arrival dates for product deliveries, which are regular and predictable. However, product content (corresponding to the coaches) is dynamic and evolves with an improved understanding of technical progress, customer requirements, and company strategy.

The roadmap contains both approved, in-production projects and future content for which dates are more tentative. Different levels of confidence can be indicated by different colors.

The roadmap is continuously updated as a rolling forecast. DPM shortens product iterations, advances content upgrades, and encourages customer interactions. One of the key features of the roadmap is that it illustrates these dynamic characteristics of portfolios.[11]

In the *Bargery Fabrics* portfolio, the roadmap illustrates a number of important issues. For example, since *Bargery Fabrics* has an aging portfolio, early income from new products is a strategic priority. Since the roadmap shows which products have an early delivery schedule, one can immediately answer the question: Does the portfolio generate early income?

The roadmap highlights the importance of marketing activities as a means of focusing technical development. For example, strategically timed marketing studies can determine whether intermediate products might be viable as stand-alone products that produce revenue.

The roadmap also exposes dependencies between products and their underlying technology platforms. Strategically important platforms are those that support multiple products. Explicitly indicating the technology platforms on the roadmap shows where early successes from one product might be transferable to another. Also, products with common technology platforms can share, not only technological developments, but marketing data.

Finally, the roadmap identifies important product milestones, such as user trials and the product launch, which is where the income begins to flow in. Thus, the roadmap explicitly links the product strategy to the financial picture.

In summary, the additional activities of DPM complete the PPM activities by providing a formal process for assessing the portfolio and ensuring that it is consistent with the company's strategic goals.

8.3.3 The Selection Funnel

The selection funnel is the metaphor often invoked to illustrate the selection of projects. In DPM, the metaphor is modified slightly to depict the selection of *ideas*, which turn into product content. This is illustrated in Fig. 8.2.

[11]Unlike projects, which do not interact.

93

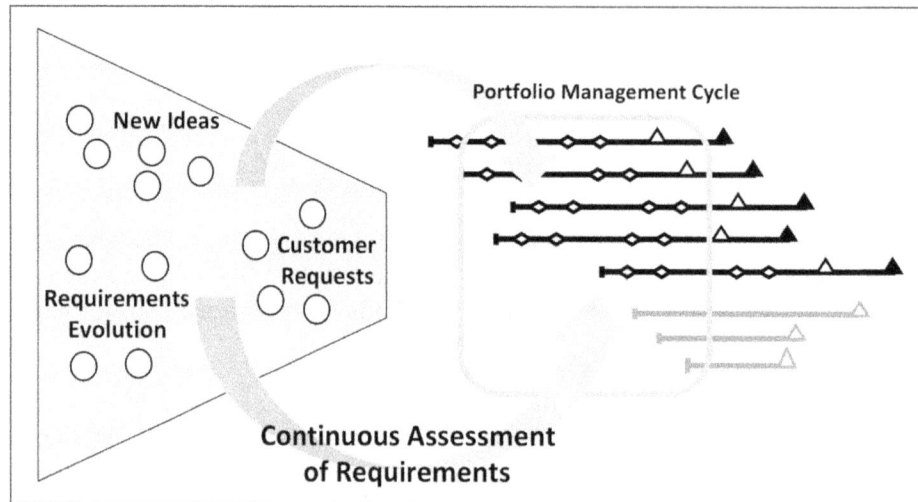

Figure 8.2: The funneling of ideas into the portfolio selection process.

8.3.4   The Role of Senior Management

In the best companies, senior managers are engaged in all aspects of portfolio management.[12] Cooper and Edgett demonstrate that senior managers have a significant impact on the success of the new product development process. [14]

Figure 8.3: The impact of senior management.

[12]This is clearly illustrated in the Panaz case, see section 6.1.

Fig. 8.3 summarizes the impact that senior managers have, and the roles they play, during the new product development process. In the best companies, senior manages are more involved in a wider variety of roles than managers in poorer performing companies.

8.3.5 Portfolio Timescales

In analyzing the timescale of portfolio changes, typical examples to look for, over the period of about a year, include:

- *Rare Changes:* Major Organizational restructuring and changes in business strategies.

- *Few Significant Changes:* New contracts with customers.

- *Several Changes:* Project delays.

- *Many Changes:* Product content changes.

While the last two items are important, the final item is the most significant.

8.4 Blue Ocean Strategy

Blue Ocean Strategy is a recent research development that updates and completely validates both Cooper's original research in Product Portfolio Management and the Petit and Hobbs research in Dynamic Portfolio Management. [15]

The goal of a blue ocean strategy is to create and capture a new type of demand.

Blue oceans represent industries not yet in existence. They have uncontested market spaces and make the competition irrelevant.

Red oceans represent industries that compete in an existing market space.

In a red ocean a company attempts to beat the competition by exploiting existing demand, the business space is well defined, and the competitive rules are known and understood. Companies try to obtain a greater market share of an existing demand. As the space gets more and more crowded, profits are harder to achieve and "cutthroat competition turns the red ocean bloody." ([15], p. 4)

In contrast to a red ocean, a blue ocean is defined by an untapped market space, the creation of a new demand, and opportunities for highly profitable growth. In

95

blue oceans, "competition is irrelevant because the rules of the game are waiting to be set." ([15], p. 5)

Table 8.2 summarizes the characteristics of red and blue oceans.

Table 8.2: The characteristics of red oceans and blue oceans.

Red Ocean	Blue Ocean
Defend Current Position	**Innovate & Pursue New Opportunities**
• Compete in existing markets	• Create uncontested markets
• Known rules	• No rules
• Cutthroat competition	• Competition irrelevant
• Demand fought over	• Create the demand
• Crowded	• Untainted by competition

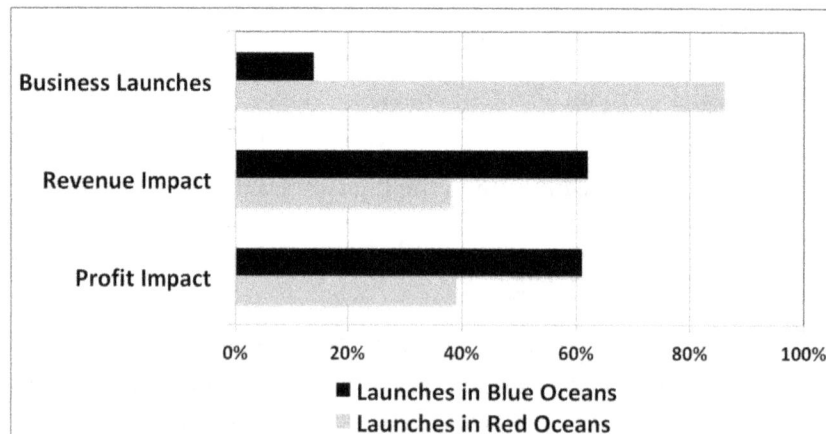

Figure 8.4: Red ocean launches dominate company performance.

Fig. 8.4 shows the dramatic differences in the impact of the introduction of blue ocean products and red ocean products. While product launches are dominated by red ocean product launches, revenues and, particularly, profits are dominated by blue ocean product launches. (Adapted from [15].)

Over 85% of new products were introduced into red oceans. However, the remaining 15% of the products, which were launched into blue oceans, were responsible for an astonishing 62% of revenue and 61% of profits.[13]

The difficulty with implementing a blue ocean strategy is that there is no simple,

[13]This dramatically reinforces the importance of Cooper's *unique and differentiated* CSF.

96

obvious way to create an innovative product that redefines the market.[14] However, a number of concepts help to create blue ocean products:

- Blue ocean strategy focuses a company's efforts on developing the product's characteristics that do not exist and that could create a blue ocean. Also, factors that are taken for granted should be eliminated or, at least not prioritized.

- Cooper's research emphasizes that the first goal should be to create a unique and differentiated product. This immediately points the portfolio towards the blue ocean.

- The research of Petit and Hobbs stresses the dynamic nature of portfolios. Shorter product life cycles and increased interaction with customers continually reinforce the goals of uniqueness and differentiation.

As an interesting example of blue ocean thinking, consider the following from *Blue Ocean Strategy* (p. 67).

> Take movie theaters. The ease and cost of getting a babysitter and parking the car affect the perceived value of going to the movies. Yet these complimentary services are beyond the bounds of the movie theater industry as it has been traditionally defined. Few cinema operators worry about how hard or costly it is for people to get babysitters. But they should, because it affects demand for their business. Imagine a movie theater with a babysitting service.
>
> Untapped value is often hidden in complementary products and services. The key is to define the total solution the buyers seek.

In summary, *Blue Ocean Strategy* completely validates the underlying research in *Dynamic Portfolio Management*.

8.5 Relation to Financial Portfolios

In the finance industry, dynamic portfolio management is a technique for managing a group of assets, such as stocks and bonds, and assessing their risks. In a financial portfolio, the assets are usually independent instruments, which diversifies the risk. However, in a *product* portfolio, the new products are rarely independent: they inherently share the same company processes, technology platforms, marketing data, and staff.

[14]Ironically, there is plenty of research that explains how to compete in a red ocean.

This makes *product* portfolio management significantly different from *financial* portfolio management. Therefore the techniques of financial portfolio management are not readily transferable to new product portfolios.

8.6 Further Reading

The first part of this case covers what is generally referred to as Product Portfolio Management (PPM) and is founded on the research of Robert Cooper, which is carefully described in *Winning at New Products*. [1] The book is eminently readable and the concepts are accessible and easily implemented in companies.

For readers who wish to learn the essence of portfolio management, we recommend *Winning at New Products* as a single, easy-to-read, source of everything the reader needs on PPM. It will also serve as an excellent reference in the future. The book contains many easily understandable charts that convincingly demonstrate the important concepts.

Cooper and his business partner, Scott Edgett, maintain a website that contains many articles about PPM in varying technical depth (http://www.prod-dev.com). The reader can easily find materials that address a particular concern or topic. However, these articles often cover the same materials that are in *Winning at New Products*.

As well as defining the critical success factors, Cooper also proposed the process by which portfolios are managed, which is called *Stage-Gate*®.

Portfolio Management For New Products is an excellent complement to *Winning at New Products*. [10] The book presents Cooper's field-tested, step-by-step framework and provides methods to assess a portfolio; to determine which products to pursue; to design and implement a portfolio management process; and to recognize and solve challenges as they arise. The second edition reports on the latest research; offers new insights on gathering and analyzing data; and showcases the practices of product market leaders.

In *Project Portfolios in Dynamic Environments*, Petit and Hobbs explain why portfolios are dynamic and define the processes necessary to manage the changes and uncertainties that occur. Petit and Hobbs also introduce a significant innovation: the product roadmap, which defines how the products combine into a coherent strategy for the portfolio.

However, unlike Cooper's *Winning at New Products* is a research monograph and we do not recommend it for general reading. Therefore, in section 8.3, we provided a brief overview of the essential aspects of Petit and Hobbs's research.

The book, *Blue Ocean Strategy* completely covers the topic with an excellent collection of examples. It also provides comprehensive support for the importance of launching a product into a blue ocean. [15] The only drawback to *Blue Ocean Strategy* is that it is light on explaining precisely how to develop such a strategy.[15]

[15]Most advice on creative strategies eventually comes to a point where one must "insert brilliant idea here!"

BIBLIOGRAPHY

[1]   Robert G. Cooper. *Winning at New Products, Creating New Products Through Innovation.* Basic Books, New York, NY, 4th edition, 2011.

[2]   Yvan Petit and Brian Hobbs. *Project Portfolios in Dynamic Environments: Organizing for Uncertainty.* Project Management Institute, Newtown Square, PA, USA., 2012.

[3]   Roger Warburton and Vijay Kanabar. *The Art and Science of Project Management.* RW Press, LLC, Newport, RI. USA., 2nd edition, 2015.

[4]   P. Rosenzweig. *The Halo Effect.* 1st Free Press, New York, NY, 2007.

[5]   E.L. Thorndike. A constant error in psychological ratings. *Journal of Applied Psychology*, 4(1):25–29, 1920.

[6]   C. Rosenstock. Project portfolio management tools and techniques. In *PMI Annual Seminars and Symposium, San Antonio, TX*, Newtown Square, PA, 2002. PMI.

[7]   Project Management Institute. *A Guide to the Project Management Body of Knowledge.* Project Management Institute, Newtown Square, PA, USA., 5th edition, 2013.

[8]   Robert G. Cooper. From Experience: The Invisible Success Factors in Product Innovation. *Journal of Product Innovation Management*, 16(2):115–133, 1999.

[9]   Robert G. Cooper, Scott J. Edgett, and J. Kleinschmidt. Portfolio management in new product development: Lessons for the leader–ii. *Research-Technology Management*, 40(6):43–52, 1997.

[10] Robert G. Cooper, Scott J. Edgett, and J. Kleinschmidt. *Portfolio Management for New Products.* New York, NY. Basic Books, 2nd edition, 2002.

[11] D.J. Teece. *Dynamic Capabilities and Strategic Management: Organizing for Innovation and Growth.* Oxford University Press, New York, NY, 2009.

[12] Robert G. Cooper. What's next?: After stage-gate. *Research-Technology Management*, 57(1):20–31, 2014.

[13] Kent Beck, Mike Beedle, Arie van Bennekum, Alistair Cockburn, Ward Cunningham, Martin Fowler, James Grenning, Jim Highsmith, Andrew Hunt, Ron Jeffries, Jon Kern, Brian Marick, Robert C. Martin, Steve Mellor, Ken Schwaber, Jeff Sutherland, and Dave Thomas. Manifesto for Agile Software Development. Technical report, agilemanifesto.org, 2001.

[14] Robert G. Cooper and Scott J. Edgett. Benchmarking best practices: Performance results and the role of senior management. Technical Report 32, Product Development Institute, 2014.

[15] W. C. Kim and R. Mauborgne. *Blue Ocean Strategy*. Harvard Business School Publishing Co., Boston, MA. USA., 2015.

[16] Lars Madsen. *Various chapter styles for the memoir class*. MemoirChapStyles.pdf, 2009.

[17] Peter Wilson and Lars Madsen. *The Memoir Class for Configurable Typesetting: User Guide*. The Herries Press, Normandy Park, WA, 8th edition, August 2009.

INDEX

Colophon

This book is set in Computer Modern Roman, 11 point size using the LaTeX typesetting system created by Leslie Lamport. The layout follows the *memoir* class with Lars Madsen's chapter styles. [16] Acknowledgments go to Peter Wilson for creating the memoir class and to Lars Madsen for maintaining it. [17] And of course, none of this would be possible without Donald Knuth who wrote the original TeX. The bibliography was produced in BibDesk. LaTeX produced the final POSTSCRIPT file that was sent to the printer.

www.ingramcontent.com/pod-product-compliance
Lightning Source LLC
Chambersburg PA
CBHW081508200326
41518CB00015B/2421